1500+ KeyWords
For $100,000+ Jobs

Books by Wendy S. Enelow

100 Winning Resumes For $100,000+ Jobs

201 Winning Cover Letters For $100,000+ Jobs

1500+ KeyWords For $100,000+ Jobs

Resume Winners From the Pros

1500+ KEYWORDS FOR $100,000+ JOBS

Wendy S. Enelow, CPRW

IMPACT PUBLICATIONS
Manassas Park, VA

1500+ KEYWORDS FOR $100,000+ JOBS

Library of Congress Cataloguing-in-Publication Data

Enelow, Wendy S.
   1500+ keywords for $100,000+ jobs / Wendy S. Enelow.
     p. cm.
  ISBN 1-57023-089-7 (alk. paper)
   1. Resumes (employment) 2. English language–
Glossaries, vocabularies, etc. I. Title.
HF5383.E478   1998
808'.06665–dc21   97-51728
                                        CIP

For information on quantity discounts, please call (703/361-7300), fax (703/335-9486), or write to: Sales Department, Impact Publications, 9104-N Manassas Drive, Manassas Park, VA 20111-5211. Distributed to the trade by National Book Network, 15200 NBN Way, Blue Ridge Summit, PA 17214, Tel. 1-800-462-6420.

CONTENTS

CHAPTER 3
**Action Verbs, High-Impact Phrases
and Personality Descriptors** **195**

ACKNOWLEDGEMENTS

Sending my heartfelt thanks and appreciation to:

... All of my clients, from whom I have learned so much about specific industries, professions, technologies, markets, management disciplines and more. I am proud to boast of the most talented pool of executive clients ever earned by any resume service. Continued success to all of you.

... All of my colleagues at the Professional Association of Resume Writers for your continued support over all of these years. I thank each and every one of you.

... Rebecca Stokes, Jeff Suter and Debi Councell for your editorial and production assistance. This book would not be possible without each of you.

... Jay A. Block, my friend, confidante and long-time supporter. We're getting there!

... My husband, David, and my son, Pierre, for the sacrifices you make because of my business, the time it takes me away from you, and the never-ending love and support you constantly show me. You guys are great!

1500+ KEYWORDS
FOR $100,000+ JOBS

CHAPTER 1

1500+ KEYWORDS

- You talk to a resume professional, recruiter, career counselor or executive coach, and each of them talks of the importance of ***KeyWords***.

- You read about the Internet and online job search, and the emphasis is on ***KeyWords*** and ***KeyWord Scanning***.

- You listen to a CNN news brief about the latest employment trends, and the reporter highlights the importance of ***KeyWords*** in today's competitive job search market.

- You attend a job search training and networking seminar, and the focus is on ***KeyWords***.

- You purchase a book on resume writing and executive career management, and the focus is on ***KeyWords*** and their importance in the development of resumes, cover letters, broadcast letters and other job search communications.

What are ***KeyWords*** and how do I find them?

Which ***KeyWords*** are right for me and my profession?

Which ***KeyWords*** are appropriate for my industry?

Where do I put ***KeyWords*** in my resume and cover letter?

You are now holding the answer to all of these questions and more about KeyWords and the tremendous impact that have in today's job search market. *__1500+ KeyWords__* is the first definitive text on the subject, detailing hundreds and hundreds of KeyWords for specific industries, professions and job functions. This book is easy to use, breaking down KeyWords for 26 major professions — from Sales to Finance, Association Management to Engineering, Real Estate to Healthcare and so much more.

__1500+ KeyWords__ is presented in four distinct sections addressing each of the four topics. Use this toolkit to identify the KeyWords appropriate to your profession, select the Action Verbs that most clearly demonstrate the caliber of your performance, and highlight the Personality Descriptors that best exemplify your leadership, management and communications style. Then review the section on High-Impact Phrases to determine how best to integrate them all to create high-powered resumes, cover letters, broadcast letters and other job search communications guaranteed to win in today's competitive domestic and international job search markets.

SECTION I

What Are KeyWords and Where Did They Come From?

Keywords are buzz words — the "hot" words associated with a specific industry, profession or job function — that clearly and succinctly communicate a specific message. KeyWords were originally defined as nouns only ... words such as benefits plan design (*for Human Resources*), market share ratings (*for Marketing & Sales*), logistics management (*for Transportation*) and platform architecture (*for Information Technology*).

Today, the definition of KeyWords has been expanded to include what we will refer to as Action Verbs, words used to present your qualifications, achievements and results in an "aggressive" style. Action Verbs are common nouns such as organized, delivered, led, negotiated, transacted, designed, conceived, imagined, created, reengineered and revitalized. No longer is a passive approach to resume writing the acceptable norm.

Trends today, influenced greatly by the tremendous competition in job search, require that resumes present your skills and qualifications in an action-driven style. Your challenge is to demonstrate the fact that you can deliver strong performance results and there is no better manner in which to accomplish this than with the use of powerful words and phrases that clearly demonstrate your capabilities.

KeyWord Scanning

KeyWords are also the standard by which thousands and thousands of companies and recruiters screen applicant resumes to identify core skills and competencies. Using advanced word scanning technology, resumes are electronically searched for the KeyWords appropriate to a company's specific hiring criteria. As such, it is critical that you include these KeyWords into your resume. If not, you will be passed over. Whether this strategy for reviewing applicant qualifications is appropriate or not, the fact remains that KeyWord scanning has become an increasingly dominant tool in today's recruitment market.

Do not allow yourself to be passed over because you do not have the "right" words in your resume. Use this text to identify those words and integrate them into your resumes and cover letters as appropriate. Not only will you meet the technological requirements of KeyWord scanning, you will also create powerful career marketing tools. And we all know that the winners in job search are those that effectively "sell" their qualifications, get noticed from the crowd of applicants and get in the door for interviews.

A sample listing of KeyWords for specific professions includes:

Profession	*KeyWord*
Accounting	Cost Accounting
Administration	Office Management
Association Management	Member Retention
Banking	Credit Administration
Customer Service	Customer Loyalty
Engineering	Project Management
Finance	Treasury Administration

Profession	_KeyWord_
General Management	Profit & Loss Management
Healthcare	Clinical Services
Hospitality	Food & Beverage Operations
Human Resources	Compensation Administration
Human Services	Client Advocacy
Information Technology	Client/Server
International Business	Emerging Markets
Law & Legal Affairs	Intellectual Property
Manufacturing	Process Automation
Marketing	Competitive Market Intelligence
PR & Communications	Crisis Communications
Purchasing	Logistics Management
Real Estate	Industrial Development
Retail	Multi-Site Operations
Sales	New Product Introduction
Security	VIP Protection
Senior Management	World Class Organization
Teaching & Education	Curriculum Development
Transportation	Traffic Management

A minor change to a KeyWord can significantly alter its meaning.

KeyWord: Sales Negotiations
Message: Negotiate customer sales contracts, pricing, terms and conditions.

KeyWord: Executive Negotiations
Message: Negotiate directly with top-level decision makers.

KeyWord: International Negotiations
Message: Negotiate with international customers, vendors and suppliers.

Using KeyWords in Resumes & Cover Letters

KeyWords can be used in developing both your resume and your cover letter(s). But first, you must know what the KeyWords are for your specific industry, job function and career path. To use this resource guide most effectively, select the profession in Chapter Two that is most related to your professional experience and current career objectives. Carefully review the KeyWords and their use, selecting all of those that are appropriate to your experience, training, track record of performance and professional credentials. Then, be sure to integrate each of them into your resume and/or cover letter.

Many of these KeyWords can be used to develop job descriptions, highlight your career achievements and identify your core competencies. Others are most appropriate when used in your Summary, Career Profile or Executive Profile (section at the beginning of your resume that highlights your core competencies, achievements and successes).

KeyWords can also be used in developing your cover letters, broadcast letters, thank you letters and other job search communications by strengthening the presentation of your skills, qualifications and experience. Use KeyWords to highlight your competencies and achievements that most relate to a specific hiring company or advertisement. If a corporation requests an individual with strong qualifications in customer service management, be sure that you highlight that specific terminology (aka KeyWord) in your resume, cover letter and other job search marketing tools. Do not expect a prospective employer to search through your resume to identify that skill. Employers generally do not spend the time nor exert the energy to analyze your resume and extrapolate your relevant skills. Spell it out clearly with the appropriate KeyWord and Action Verb presentation.

SECTION II

What Are Action Verbs?

Action Verbs are a select group of verbs that allow you to present your qualifications, competencies, achievements, performance results and KeyWords in an "aggressive" and "action-driven" style. They are "common" words, like accelerated, achieved, captured, delivered, drove, increased, managed, negotiated, produced, strategized, won and more.

Using Action Verbs in Resumes & Cover Letters

Action Verbs are best used as the first word in a sentence in either your resume or cover letter(s). Accepting the fact that most resumes are written in the first person with the "I" omitted, you would state "Saved (ACTION VERB) the company over $250,000 in annual payroll costs through internal restaffing and training initiatives" instead of "I saved the company ..."

Action Verbs create a sense of immediacy and top-level achievement. They communicate that you deliver results, improve performance, provide strong leadership, and orchestrate complex functions and operations. Several examples include:

- Spearheaded start-up and global market launch of new telecommunications division, now a $450 million revenue center and the fastest growing division in the corporation.

- Structured and negotiated a complex joint venture between U.S. and Japanese business partners.

- Revitalized manufacturing operations, implemented stringent inventory controls, automated previously manual functions, and reduced annual costs by 34%.

- Captured a 12% gain in market share despite intense competition and economic instability.

SECTION III

The remainder of this book is divided into two chapters:

Chapter 2 - KeyWords By Profession

KeyWords By Profession is a comprehensive listing of more than 1000 KeyWords for 22 major career fields. Each KeyWord is presented in a sentence to better understand its use and the message it conveys to your reader.

Chapter 3 - Action Verbs, High-Impact Phrases & Personality Descriptors

This Chapter includes more than 500 Action Verbs, High-Impact Phrases and Personality Descriptors for use in developing resume and cover letter content. Review these lists carefully, select those most appropriate to your career, qualifications, experience and performance, and incorporate them into your resume and cover letters.

NOTE FROM THE AUTHOR:

No word listing is comprehensive. This book has been prepared to provide you with a starting point upon which to build. Feel free to add in your own KeyWords, Action Verbs, High-Impact Phrases and Personality Descriptors.

Good Luck!
May The Best Resume Win!

CHAPTER 2

KeyWords By Profession

Administration
Association & Not-For-Profit Management
Banking
Customer Service
Engineering
Finance, Accounting & Auditing
General Management, Senior Management & Consulting
Healthcare
Hospitality
Human Resources
Human Services
Information Systems & Telecommunications Technology
International Business Development
Law & Corporate Legal Affairs
Manufacturing & Operations Management
Public Relations & Corporate Communications
Purchasing & Logistics
Real Estate, Construction & Property Management
Retail
Sales & Marketing
Security & Law Enforcement
Teaching & Educational Administration
Transportation

ADMINISTRATION

Positions

Administrative Assistant
Administrative Director
Administrator
Corporate Secretary
Executive Assistant
Executive Secretary
Manager of Administrative Services
Office Administrator
Office Assistant
Office Coordinator
Office Manager
Office Services Manager
Secretary to President
Vice President of Administration

KeyWords

Administration - Appointed Senior **Administration** Director responsible for office affairs, messenger services, equipment acquisition and allocation, records management, courier services and headquarters facilities operations.

Administrative Infrastructure - Streamlined **administrative infrastructure**, integrated similar functions, reduced staffing requirements and saved over $200,000 annually.

Administrative Processes - Redesigned **administrative processes** to streamline functions, eliminate redundancy and expedite workflow.

Administrative Support - Provided high-level **administrative support** and managed organizational liaison affairs for the President, CEO and CFO.

Back Office Operations - Reorganized **back office operations** for a 22-branch banking network, reduced daily settlement time by one hour and redesigned to branch reporting system.

Budget Administration - Retained accountability for all administrative and office management operations while assuming additional responsibility for **budget administration** for 16 individual cost centers throughout the corporation.

Client Communications - Designed, wrote and directed production of advertisements, promotions, marketing collaterals, sales materials and other **client communications**.

Confidential Correspondence - Prepared **confidential correspondence** for CEO's signature.

Contract Administration - Directed **contract administration** affairs for over $22 million in contractual and legal agreements with business associates nationwide.

Corporate Recordkeeping - Responsible for **corporate recordkeeping** of all Board meeting minutes and agendas.

Corporate Secretary - Appointed **Corporate Secretary** to the Board of Directors.

Customer Liaison - Served as the direct **customer liaison** to $1+ million accounts.

Document Management - Designed recordkeeping, reporting and **document management** systems to streamline workflow and enhance accountability.

Efficiency Improvement - Spearheaded a series of reorganization initiatives for **efficiency improvement**, productivity gain and quality improvement.

Executive Liaison Affairs - Managed **executive liaison affairs** on behalf of the senior executive team.

Executive Officer Support - Coordinated meeting planning, conference scheduling, travel and transportation arrangements to **support executive officers**.

Facilities Management - Directed **facilities management**, use and resource allocation for six manufacturing plants throughout Kentucky and Tennessee.

Front Office Operations - Trained and supervised a team of 16 secretaries, clerks and support personnel managing **front office operations** at Xerox headquarters.

Government Affairs - Prepared reports, correspondence and documentation for company-wide **government affairs** and reporting functions.

Liaison Affairs - Coordinated high-level staffing functions to improve **liaison affairs** with the top 10 customers worldwide.

Mail & Messenger Services - Outsourced **mail and messenger services** to third party contractor, saving the company over $250,000 in annual operating costs.

Meeting Planning - Directed **meeting planning** for two major conferences, including conference agendas, guest speakers, logistics, travel, transportation, meals and special events.

Office Management - Promoted to **office management** position leading a staff of 14 and controlling a $300,000 annual operating budget.

Office Services - Streamlined and consolidated **office services** for 16 branches throughout the State of Maryland.

Policy & Procedure - Authored **policies and procedures** for all administrative, office services, purchasing, inventory and facilities maintenance programs.

Product Support - Worked in cooperation with Sales and Marketing teams to design improved **product support** and customer support programs.

Productivity Improvement - Introduced time and territory management processes that drove a better than 10% gain in **productivity**, quality and efficiency.

Project Management - Coordinated **project management**, personnel and resources for development of emerging multimedia technologies.

Records Management - Streamlined document flow and enhanced **records management**.

Regulatory Reporting - Managed **regulatory reporting** with local, state and government agencies.

Resource Management - Evaluated organizational needs, designed flow-charts, and directed **resource management** and allocation.

Technical Support - Provided **technical support** for specific PC applications to administrative staff worldwide.

Time Management - Created innovative **time management** systems for manufacturing, sales, marketing, order processing and administrative staffs.

Workflow Planning/Prioritization - Designed innovative **workflow planning and prioritization** strategies, resulting in a better than 25% improvement in productivity and efficiency ratings.

ROSLYN M. CHAMBERS

2395 Fair Oaks Court
Silver Spring, Maryland 22591

Home   (301) 339-4132
Office (202) 695-4208

AREA ADMINISTRATIVE MANAGER

High-Performance Administrator with 15+ years experience supporting multi-site regional sales, marketing, sales training and customer support operations. Expert organizational, leadership, teambuilding and communication skills. Recognized for professionalism, creativity, resourcefulness and competence in managing administrative affairs and supporting organizational goals.

CORE COMPETENCIES:

- Sales & Marketing Support
- Senior Staff Relations & Communications
- Vendor & Customer Communications
- Policy & Procedure Compliance
- Productivity & Performance Management
- Reporting, Recordkeeping & Documentation

- Project Planning & Management
- Special Events & Meetings Management
- Problem Solving & Decision Making
- Workload Planning & Prioritization
- Staff Training & Development
- Long-Range Business Planning

PROFESSIONAL EXPERIENCE:

RAYBURN MICROSYSTEMS, INC., Washington, D.C.   1985 to Present

Area Administrative Supervisor

Promoted through a series of increasingly responsible administrative positions supporting large-scale regional sales and customer management programs. Currently work in cooperation with Area Vice President and other senior management to plan and direct administrative affairs for the Southern Area (12 states with 125 field sales representatives). Lead a team of 12-15 field administrators. Work independently with little or no direct supervision.

Process Design & Performance Improvement

- Design and implement enhanced administrative processes, procedures and systems to support rapid regional growth ($450 million in 1994 to $830 million projected for 1997). Anticipate organizational needs and initiate appropriate actions to obtain resources, technologies and personnel to meet peak workload demands.

Operating Support

- Consult with Vice President, Human Resources Director, Controller and other senior staff to plan workload, allocate personnel, coordinate special projects and facilitate the entire administrative function. Work in cooperation with management teams to resolve problems impacting efficiency and productivity of the organization.

Management Support

- Independently direct administrative affairs on behalf of Vice President. Draft correspondence and other communications, coordinate meetings and calendar requests, prioritize incoming projects, process travel arrangements and prepare expense reports. Represent Vice President with other groups, departments and divisions.

Special Events Management

- Plan, staff, budget and manage sales meetings, conferences, leadership programs and special events. Coordinate communications with hotels, caterers, transportation companies, meeting planners, exhibitors, suppliers and speakers. Most notable event was the 1995 Southern Area Kick-Off Meeting with 300+ in attendance.

Human Resource Affairs

- Hire, train, schedule, supervise and evaluate the work performance of administrative, clerical and support personnel. Define long-term staffing requirements, coordinate staff training and development programs, and initiate disciplinary action as appropriate. Participate in annual performance reviews and long-range career planning/direction.

Facilities Management

- Coordinate office relocations, consolidations and renovation projects to accommodate growth and new hires. Redesign existing space layouts to enhance efficiency and ensure optimum utilization of all physical resources. Manage cable, telecommunications, security and other systems installations. Saved $6300 on proposed $7000 fire systems upgrade project through strategic negotiations and vendor management.

Purchasing Management

- Plan and direct purchasing programs for office equipment, services, supplies and furnishings. Source new vendors, negotiate pricing and discounts, coordinate logistics and maintain inventory levels. Currently manage purchasing operations through corporate headquarters.

Financial Affairs

- Maintain $11,000 checking account, reconcile petty cash accounts and prepare informal financial statements for review by senior management. Justify increased spending to meet operating, staffing, facilities and administrative requirements.

RRT DEVELOPMENT CORPORATION, Alexandria, Virginia   1972 to 1985

Fast-track promotion from Receptionist to Order Operations Clerk to Administrative Assistant to Director of DoD Sales to**Executive Assistant to Vice President of Federal Sales Systems Group**. Managed all administrative support functions for a 200+ person field sales organization. Trained/supervised less experienced administrative staff.

- Participated in a series of internal change and process redesign initiatives to improve the efficiency of order processing, data entry, proposal preparation, sales administration and customer service/support.

EDUCATION & CAREER TRAINING:

- Frontline Leadership
- Business As Usual Seminar
- Career Architect Planning
- Managing Field Compensation
- Sexual Harassment & Performance Management
- Time Management & Conflict Management

ASSOCIATION & NOT-FOR-PROFIT MANAGEMENT

Positions

Agency Director

Association Director

Board Director

Certified Association Executive (CAE)

Chairperson/Chairman

Chief Administrative Officer (CAO)

Chief Executive Officer (CEO)

Chief Financial Officer (CFO)

Chief Operating Officer (COO)

Committee Chairperson

Committee Member

Executive Director

Foundation Chairperson/Chairman

Fundraiser

Legislative Affairs Officer

Marketing Director

Media Relations Officer

Membership Development Manager

Political Affairs Officer

President

Public Policy Director

Research Director

Special Events Director

Vice President

KeyWords

Advocacy - Orchestrated a large member **advocacy** program designed to reduce regulatory oversight over industry-specific operations.

Affiliate Members - Expanded membership to include **affiliate members** of primary vendors, contractors and subcontractors to the association.

Board Relations - Managed high-profile **board relations** and presentations, with an emphasis on increasing corporate giving and annual funding.

Budget Allocation - Directed **budget allocation** and reporting functions for the association and its 210 nationwide chapter organizations.

Budget Oversight - Led management team responsible for **budget oversight** and administration of over $50 million in annual funding.

Chapter - Established **chapter** network to expand member services and increase the sale of member products, training, seminars and other revenue-generating programs.

Community Outreach - Spearheaded design and development of advertising and promotional materials to expand **community outreach** and support continued operation of community centers and recreational programs.

Corporate Development - Guided executive management team in the conceptualization, design and execution of targeted **corporate development** campaigns.

Corporate Giving - Expanded **corporate giving** campaigns throughout regional and national communities.

Corporate Sponsorship - Negotiated $2 million **corporate sponsorship** with Johnson & Johnson to fund industry training and educational opportunities.

Education Foundation - Formed an **education foundation** and funded with grant dollars from NIH, the Centers for Disease Control and several private organizations.

Educational Programming - Directed 9-person training team responsible for **educational programming**, curriculum development, classroom instruction and program certification.

Endowment Funds - Administered over $200 million in annual **endowment funds** from public and private supporters.

Foundation Management - Senior Executive with full operational responsibility for **foundation management**, funding, staffing, technology and long-range development strategy.

Fundraising - Led teams of up to 200 volunteers for the American Red Cross annual **fundraising** campaign.

Grassroots Campaign - Utilized successful **grassroots campaign** to support legislative passage of favorable family leave law.

Industry Association - Established new **industry association** to represent the interests, issues and financial needs of key players in the downtrending aerospace industry.

Industry Relations - Drove forward a high-profile **industry relations** initiative to advocate for the passage of favorable trade legislation.

Leadership Training - Designed high-performance **leadership training** programs for top-level association management nationwide.

Marketing Communications - Led creative team in the design and production of multimedia **marketing communications** for both member development and fundraising programs.

Media Relations - Appointed Association Spokesperson responsible for **media relations**, broadcast interviews and crisis communications.

Member Communications - Wrote monthly newsletters, weekly Internet memos and other **member communications** to improve member retention.

Member Development - Increased annual revenues from product sales by 34% through implementation of innovative **member development** programs and promotions.

Member-Driven Organization - Transitioned from hierarchical organization into **member-driven organization** responsive to the needs of 2000+ members and 500+ affiliate members.

Member Retention - Improved **member retention** rates 15% by expanding regular communications and increasing number of services.

Member Services - Expanded **member services** to include training programs, legislative and regulatory support, compensation models, loan financings and a group buying consortium.

Mission Planning - Assembled and facilitated 6-person industry team to guide **mission planning** and define organizational vision.

Not-For-Profit - Senior Operating Executive of **not-for-profit** industry association formed to provide marketing, financial, technological and educational support to human service organizations throughout the state of Massachusetts.

Organization(al) Leadership - Challenged to provide strong and decisive **organizational leadership** through a period of change, transition and revitalization.

Organization(al) Mission - Redefined **organizational mission** in response to changing economic and service delivery requirements.

Organization(al) Vision - Charted a clear **organizational vision** to lead the association into the year 2000.

Policy Development - Guided **policy development** in cooperation with the Board of Trustees and major corporate sponsors.

Political Affairs (Political Action Committee - PAC) - Formed and led the organization's first-ever **PAC** to meet increasingly complex legislative and regulatory requirements impacting member companies worldwide.

Press Relations - Managed high-profile **press relations** with print and broadcast media.

Public Policy Development - Led congressional staff responsible for **public policy development** and dissemination.

Public Relations - Spearheaded a winning **public relations** program targeted to corporate and industrial business partners, increasing annual funding by more than $20 million.

Public/Private Partnerships - Forged **public/private partnerships** with MIT, the University of Pittsburgh, Virginia Polytechnic and the University of Texas to manage cooperative research programs.

Regulatory Affairs - Directed all **regulatory affairs**, compliance and reporting functions to meet local, state and federal requirements for not-for-profit status.

Research Foundation - Established a joint public/private funded **research foundation** leading the nation in oncological research and drug development.

Speakers Bureau - Successfully marketed the association's **speakers bureau** to affiliate member organizations nationwide.

Special Events Management - Directed **special events management** teams responsible for production and execution of seminars, conferences, social meetings and other events throughout the year.

Volunteer Recruitment - Spearheaded a successful **volunteer recruitment** program in support of annual fundraising campaign.

Volunteer Training - Designed and led **volunteer training** in communications, recordkeeping, data entry and fundraising.

PHILLIP W. MORRISON
3204 Edgemont Place
Chevy Chase, Maryland 22351

Home (410) 669-4352   Office (410) 182-2343

NOT-FOR-PROFIT ASSOCIATION EXECUTIVE
Private Voluntary Organizations

Dynamic 10-year executive management career leading large-scale, not-for-profit organizations worldwide. Expert in evaluating organizational needs and creating proactive development, relief, service and outreach programs that have consistently achieved/surpassed operating goals.

CORE COMPETENCIES:

- Development Issues - Theory & Practice
- Fundraising & Marketing
- Multi-Site Management
- Strategic Planning & Policy Development
- Institution Building & Support
- Humanitarian Relief
- Public & Private Partnerships
- Board Relations & Donor Negotiations
- Health Care & Education Services
- Problem Solving & Decision Making

Extensive international experience with excellent knowledge of the political and social cultures, trends and operating environments in both Africa and Latin America. Strong and decisive leadership talents. Excellent analytical, organizational, mediation and cross-cultural communication skills. Fluent Spanish and French.

PROFESSIONAL EXPERIENCE:

HUMAN RELIEF SERVICES - HRS, Landover, Maryland   1973 to Present

Distinguished management career with one of the world's largest and most diversified private voluntary organizations sponsoring sustainable self-help programs in the areas of agriculture, primary health care, education, micro-credit lending and human rights. HRS is also one of the world's leaders in emergency relief assistance.

Throughout majority of tenure, served as Senior Executive of regional operations worldwide with full responsibility for strategic planning, programming, financial management, human resources, administration, marketing, resource acquisition and daily operations management. Demonstrated expertise in fundraising, cross-cultural relations, team building and leadership.

Special Assistant to the Deputy Executive Director - World Headquarters (1995 to Present)

Promoted to newly-created position and challenged to leverage resources from affiliate European organizations to expand international programming. Currently directing the development of an innovative international support program combining monetary and in-kind fundraising in cooperation with U.S. farmers and the U.S. government.

Coordinator - Domestic Outreach & Education - World Headquarters (1994 to 1995)

Created new strategy to expand cooperative efforts with the organization's 196 affiliates nationwide. Launched a portfolio of marketing, educational and communication programs to increase awareness, expand partnerships and increase program funding. Held collateral responsibility for a number of annual special events and fundraising initiatives to support worldwide operations. Planned strategies and directed efforts that raised over $14 million in annual funding.

PHILLIP W. MORRISON - *Page Two*

Regional Director - Central America & Caribbean, Nicaragua (1992 to 1994)

Senior Operating Executive directing all HRS operations in six countries and large-scale special projects in three other countries. Directed the allocation of over $25 million in annual funds to expand agricultural, primary health care, sanitation, micro-credit lending and other cutting-edge development programs in a highly-charged political environment.

- Defined programming requirements, acquired resources and assembled management team to resettle ex-combatants from both sides of the conflict following 10-year civil war in El Salvador.
- Introduced quality-driven program management and audit review processes, and unique project approval/management process to transition program "ownership" to local nationals.
- Structured, negotiated and obtained $1.3 million grant from USAID to improve water and sanitation services.

Regional Director - East Africa & the Indian Ocean, Kenya (1987 to 1992)

Senior Operating Executive leading the successful introduction of new development strategy designed in previous position. Challenged to transition strategy from concept into action, building what was the single largest field operation in HRS. High-profile position included direct responsibility for permanent operations in seven countries and major relief programs in three others. Managed $80 to $100 million in annual funding and 250+ paid staff.

- Led the largest and most sophisticated program in the 53-year history of the organization, delivering relief services to over 2.6 million displaced Ethiopians each month.
- Spearheaded development of the first-ever cross border relief programs in Somalia.
- Restructured management hierarchy throughout the nine-country region, implemented decentralized management system and created a local ownership philosophy to strengthen program commitment of both HRS and local national teams.
- Launched the successful introduction of the new Africa Development Strategy and created model for worldwide implementation over the next 10 years.

Deputy Director - Africa Region / Director - African Development Group (1985 to 1987)

Spearheaded a massive effort to redirect the focus of development programming throughout the region and build strategic partnerships with other major donor agencies worldwide. Focused new strategy on local program ownership, popular participation and institution building. Dedicated $20 million to finance implementation of new strategy in Africa.

Program Director (1977 to 1984) with assignments in Southern Africa, East Africa and Central America. Managed development and emergency relief programs for 100,000+ people.

Program Assistant (1973 to 1977) in Guatemala, Nicaragua and Ecuador.

LESTER CORPORATION, New York, New York   1970 to 1973

Financial Analyst / Assistant Cash Manager

GENERAL MOTORS, New York, New York   1969 to 1970

Financial Analyst - Corporate Treasury Department

EDUCATION: **MBA - Finance/International Business,** Columbia University Graduate School of Business
BS - Economics, Boston College

BANKING

Positions

Assistant Branch Manager
Assistant Cashier
Assistant Vice President
Bank Manager
Branch Manager
Cashier
Chief Executive Officer (CEO)
Commercial Credit Officer
Consumer Credit Officer
CRA Director
Customer Service Manager
Credit Analyst
Credit Officer
Director of Commercial Banking
Director of Consumer Banking
Director of Credit Administration
Director of Depository Services
Director of Investment
Director of Lending
Director of Retail Banking
Division Director
Executive Vice President
First Vice President
Lending Officer

Managing Director

President

Regional Vice President

Risk Manager

Second Vice President

Senior Vice President

Underwriter

Vice President

KeyWords

Asset Management - Administered NationsBank's **asset management** function, including direct control of a $2.8 billion portfolio.

Asset-Based Lending - Controlled over $6 billion in **asset-based lending** programs allocated for capital investments, acquisitions and joint venture programs of major corporate clients.

Audit Examination - Managed **audit examination** of all GE Credit operations nationwide.

Branch Operations - Senior Manager with full responsibility for staffing, service and administration of **branch operations** throughout the Ohio Delta Region.

Cash Management - Directed corporate **cash management**, treasury, foreign exchange and currency hedging programs.

Commercial Banking - Transitioned Central Fidelity from a small community bank into a major **commercial banking** center with the introduction of lending, commercial paper and credit operations.

Commercial Credit - Structured, negotiated and executed over $200 million in **commercial credit** transactions in FY95.

Consumer Banking - Expanded **consumer banking** programs to include 24-hour ATM services and 24-hour credit authorization.

Consumer Credit - Controlled a $450 million **consumer credit** portfolio, all loan authorizations and all loan recovery procedures.

Correspondent Banking - Negotiated **correspondent banking** relationships with major financial institutions throughout the Pacific Rim.

Credit Administration - Directed **credit administration** for all personal loans exceeding $50 million.

Credit Analysis - Designed bank-wide models for **credit analysis** and credit valuation.

de novo Banking - Established **de novo banking** operations to support Mellon's expansion throughout emerging Latin American markets.

Debt Financing - Structured and negotiated over $350 million in **debt financing** to ensure continued operation of GE's Appliance Sales Division.

Deposit Base - Built **deposit base** by 25% over two years, exceeding all objectives for fee income, new customers and penetration of new commercial markets.

Depository Services - Administered **depository services** for all commercial clients, real estate investment partnerships and major construction programs.

Equity Financing - Negotiated $1.2 billion in **equity financing** to fund LBO.

Fee Income - Accelerated regional expansion and increased **fee income** by 18%.

Foreign Exchange (FX) - Managed Commercial Federal's global **foreign exchange** program.

Global Banking - Senior Operating Executive with full responsibility for the strategic planning, staffing and start-up of **global banking** operations to transition First National from a domestic institution into a worldwide player in the financial arena.

Investment Management - Directed **investment management**, allocation and reporting of all general and limited partnership programs for American Saving's Real Estate Division.

Investor Relations - Authored and published monthly communications to strengthen **investor relations** and support the bank's long-range expansion objectives.

Lease Administration - Designed and directed **lease administration** programs for advanced information, electronics and telecommunications equipment.

Letters of Credit - Negotiated $800 million in **letters of credit** to fund international commodities trading.

Liability Exposure - Reduced **liability exposure** with the introduction of more stringent lending and credit authorization procedures.

Loan Administration - Managed **loan administration**, documentation and regulatory reporting functions in support of headquarters and branch operations.

Loan Processing - Directed 12-person professional and administrative support staff responsible for **loan processing** and documentation.

Loan Quality - Introduced improved internal controls, credit analysis and credit administration procedures to enhance **loan quality** and performance.

Loan Recovery - Directed **loan recovery** of more than $300 million in outstanding credits.

Loan Underwriting - Managed department responsible for **loan underwriting** and analysis of customer creditworthiness.

Lockbox Processing - Managed night shift **lockbox processing** and funds transfer operations.

Merchant Banking - Direct liaison between MNB, VISA, MasterCard, American Express and Discover to coordinate all **merchant banking** and reporting functions.

Non-Performing Assets - Restored the institution's liquidity with the recovery of over $480 million in **non-performing assets**.

Portfolio Management - Directed **portfolio management** for venture capital and investor lending programs.

Receivership - Appointed CEO to manage the institution through **receivership** and projected turnaround/asset workout.

Regulatory Affairs - Facilitated all **regulatory affairs**, reporting and compliance programs for a multi-site banking operation.

Relationship Management - Focused service staffs on building and strengthening the institution's **relationship management** programs with large retail and commercial customers.

Retail Banking - Built and managed the region's #1 ranked **retail banking** firm (based on quality of service, ease in lending/credit and staff performance).

Retail Lending - Expanded **retail lending** into non-traditional customer markets and increased loan portfolio by $120 million in first year.

Return-On-Assets (ROA) - Structured and negotiated divestiture of all bank operations in Southern Texas and delivered 34% **ROA**.

Return-On-Equity (ROE) - Designed loan administration and recovery programs that increased the bank's **ROE** performance by an average of 12% annually.

Return-On-Investment (ROI) - Acquired a small community bank, expanded services and programs, and divested in 1994 for a 23% **ROI** to principal investor group.

Risk Management - Spearheaded design and implementation of an aggressive **risk management** program that, over the next 10 years, reduced bad debt portfolio by over $2 billion.

Secondary Markets - Directed loan sales throughout **secondary markets** in the U.S. and Canada.

Secured Lending - Restructured **secured lending** programs to reduce exposure and improve recovery.

Securities Management - Recruited to ASB America to build and direct their first **securities management** operation.

Transaction Banking - Senior Officer specializing in **transaction banking** for major corporate loans and credits.

Trust Services - Administered the bank's **trust services** program and over $750 million in trust funds.

Unsecured Lending - Expanded loan programs to include **unsecured lending** for preferred customer base.

Wholesale Banking - Introduced **wholesale banking** services to accelerate growth and diversification.

Workout - Directed an aggressive loan **workout** department that restructured and recovered 89% of outstanding debt.

RICHARD W. JACKSON

4014 Davidson Lane	Home	(358) 208-9256
St. Louis, Missouri 60604	Office	(358) 488-3478
	E-Mail	RWJ@netlink.com

COMMUNITY BANKING EXECUTIVE

Strategic Planning / Banking Services & Products / Sales & Marketing / Deposit Growth
Commercial & Consumer Lending / Mortgage Lending / Credit Administration / Workout & Recovery
MIS Technology / Finance & Budgeting / Human Resources / Multi-Site Operations Management

Dynamic professional career leading banking institutions through start-up, turnaround, merger, acquisition and growth. Delivered strong and sustainable gains in revenue, fee income and asset value within highly competitive and volatile markets. Excellent planning, organizational development and leadership qualifications. Expert negotiator, spokesperson and change agent. Able to effectively communicate high-level technical and financial information to nontechnical audiences.

PROFESSIONAL EXPERIENCE:

President	**WESTERN GLOBE CORP.**	1993 to 1995

Transitioned career out of banking and into a commercial enterprise to accelerate growth of this natural gas marketing company following deregulation and entry into a competitive business market. Given full autonomy for identifying and capitalizing upon opportunities to recreate Western Globe as diversified energy provider to industrial and commercial customers.

- Nurtured relationships with previous business colleagues and associates to launch Western Globe's successful entry into the commercial energy markets. Delivered 100% revenue growth within less than two years.
- Spearheaded selection and implementation of fully-integrated MIS technology to automate all core business functions.

President & CEO	**FINANCIAL FEDERAL**	1988 to 1993

Appointed President & CEO following the merger of Myers Bank, State Bank and Tress Federal to create Financial Federal. Challenged to lead the new organization through an aggressive reorganization, turnaround and return to profitability.

Held P&L responsibility for the institution and all business units (e.g., Lending, Mortgage Banking, Funds Acquisition, Sales/Marketing, Human Resources, MIS, Operations, Finance and Budgeting, Strategic Planning, Customer Service). Led six-person senior management team.

- Met/exceeded all turnaround objectives for this $750 million savings and loan. Consolidated 660 employees in 59 locations in 7 states to 420 employees in 23 locations throughout Missouri. Transitioned from 1987 loss of $21 million to 1990 earnings of $8+ million.
- Orchestrated the workout and recovery of over $60 million in non-performing assets.
- Created, launched and marketed a series of consumer, mortgage and small commercial lending programs to reestablish the institution and rebuild solvent portfolio.
- Repositioned the new institution within the marketplace, restored confidence within the consumer and commercial communities, and launched a well-targeted marketing and public relations campaign to rebuild market image.

NOTE: Appointed Co-Director to facilitate two-year transition and integration of operations following Prairie Bancorp's acquisition of Financial Federal in 1991.

RICHARD W. JACKSON   *Page Two*

Vice President of Administration	MYERS BANK F.S.B.	1982 to 1988

Member of five-person executive management team leading the transition of Federal Savings & Loan Association into a publicly-owned federal savings bank (Myers). Redesigned organizational infrastructure, reengineered operations and guided the institution through a period of rapid growth and diversification. Led strategic planning and market repositioning.

Directed the Administration Division (MIS, Human Resources, General Services) with 30 employees and a $5 million annual budget. Created dynamic business processes, operations, policies and procedures to meet changing organizational needs.

- Recreated Federal through an aggressive merger and acquisition program with six other institutions to create newly-formed Myers Bank.
- Instrumental in building assets from $140 million to $680 million, expanding locations from 7 to 47 and increasing employee base from 100 to 500.

Vice President of Management Systems	FEDERAL SAVINGS & LOAN	1977 to 1982

Promoted from Management Systems Specialist to Vice President within two years. Evaluated organizational needs and facilitated design/implementation of improved operating and administrative processes impacting all key business units. Concurrent responsibility for spearheading a number of new programs and services to diversify the bank's portfolio.

- Invested over $2 million in technology upgrades to automate and upgrade operating processes. Led conversion from service bureau to in-house information systems.
- Guided the development of operating, administrative and back office procedures for the start-up of the first retail banking network in the State of Missouri.
- Orchestrated development, staffing, budgeting and start-up of property management company to expand statewide real estate practice.
- Introduced new cash management program, space management systems, security training program and a portfolio of other internal processes.
- Directed construction of four retail deposit facilities. Brought project in on time and within budget despite construction overrides and accelerating costs.
- Recognized nationally for expertise in systems automation and back office processing by U.S. Savings & Loan League.

Director of Claims Processing	MISSOURI WORKER'S COMP.	1974 to 1977

Member of five-person management team challenged to reengineer and modernize the operations, processes and technologies of this $54 million fund (80,000+ claims annually). Directed implementation of automated claims processing systems, redesigned core business systems, developed training programs, and supervised 100+ personnel through seven direct management reports.

MIS Consultant	CMB, INC.	1973 to 1974
Teaching / Research Assistant	NATIONAL SCIENCE FOUNDATION	1972

EDUCATION: MISSOURI STATE UNIVERSITY
MS Degree (Industrial Engineering), 1974
BS Degree (Industrial Engineering), 1972

OUACHITA TECHNICAL COLLEGF

CUSTOMER SERVICE

Positions

Account Manager
Account Representative
Account Services Coordinator
Customer Acceptance Representative
Customer Loyalty Manager
Customer Service Liaison
Customer Service Manager
Customer Service Representative
Director of Account Relations
Director of Customer Service
Director Sales Support & Delivery
Key Account Manager
Key Account Service Manager
Sales Administrator
Sales Support Administrator
Telemarketing Manager
Telemarketing Representative
Vice President of Customer Service & Retention

KeyWords

Account Relationship Management - Directed all customer service functions for major **account relationship management** and development projects.

Customer Communications - Created a complete portfolio of print, broadcast and video **customer communications** in cooperation with Sales, Marketing, Product Development and Operations.

Customer Development - Member of cross-functional team responsible for strategy, operations and service planning for new **customer development** initiatives.

Customer Focus Groups - Facilitated **customer focus groups** with large consumer groups to expand Levi's penetration into emerging seniors' market.

Customer Loyalty - Championed development and global market launch of IBM's first-ever **customer loyalty** programs to retain competitive market lead.

Customer Management - Drove forward innovative **customer management** initiatives to expand level, scope and caliber of both in-house and field service organizations.

Customer Needs Assessment - Facilitated cross-functional teams responsible for **customer needs assessment** and service delivery.

Customer Retention - Pioneered innovative, incentive-based **customer retention** initiatives that contributed to a better than 20% gain in long-term client relationships.

Customer Satisfaction - Measured **customer satisfaction** through mail and telephone surveys, customer focus groups and email communications.

Customer Service - Credited with building a world class **customer service** organization supporting field sales and product distribution programs through 22 states in the Eastern U.S.

Customer Surveys - Designed and administered **customer surveys** to further clarify customer expectations, product and service requirements, cost objectives and competitive partnerships.

Field Service Operation - Managed a 62-person regional **field service operation** supporting IBM PC and peripherals installations.

Inbound Service Operation - Staffed a 24x7 **inbound service operation** supporting surgical implants and devices at leading healthcare research and medical centers nationwide.

Key Account Management - Supported **key account management** team with complete service, support and administration.

Order Fulfillment - Expanded **order fulfillment** operations to include off-site contractors to meet increased demand while controlling escalating costs.

Order Processing - Led a 62-person **order processing** operation to the highest levels of productivity in the 42-year history of the company.

Outbound Service Operation - Revitalized **outbound service operation**, expanded technical and training staff, introduced PCs and email communications, and restored customer credibility.

Process Simplification - Architected a company-wide **process simplification** program to streamline order entry, processing, fulfillment, billing, collection and service operations.

Records Management - Redesigned and automated customer **records management** system to more accurately track historical data, product requirements and pricing.

Relationship Management - Designed service-based **relationship management** programs to strengthen customer retention and loyalty.

Sales Administration - Directed the entire **sales administration**, budgeting and reporting function for the $5.8 million Central LA sales and service region.

Service Benchmarks - Created the industry's first-ever **service benchmarks** for Internet customer support.

Service Delivery - Redesigned **service delivery** processes, increased staff field time by 30% and improved customer satisfaction ratings 89%.

Service Measures - Introduced quantifiable **service measures** to track individual technician performance.

Service Quality - Spearheaded design and implementation of measurable **service quality** parameters to support company-wide continuous quality improvement initiative.

Telemarketing Operations - Recruited to direct the start-up of nation-wide **telemarketing operations** to complement direct and distributor sales programs.

Telesales Operations - Pioneered **telesales operations** to introduce IBM's new consumer-based technology.

NOREEN COLLINS

899 South Pacific Grove   Residence (415) 548-9721
Valley Vista, California 90898   Office   (415) 684-3145

CUSTOMER SERVICE / CONSUMER AFFAIRS / RESPONSE CENTER MANAGEMENT
Building & Directing High-Profile Customer Management Organizations

- Strategic Business Planning
- Technology Acquisition
- Vendor Sourcing / Negotiations
- Contract Development / Compliance
- Market Research / Analysis

- Customer / Client Service Management
- Multi-Site Call Center Management
- Human Resource Allocation
- Professional Training & Development
- Process / Procedure Standardization

*Built two high-profile customer response/customer management organizations that
consistently exceeded productivity, quality and customer satisfaction objectives.*

PROFESSIONAL EXPERIENCE:

SIMPSON FOODS, San Francisco, California   1984 to Present

Fast-track promotion through a series of increasingly responsible management positions leading
nationwide customer service/customer response operations of one of the largest food manufacturers in the U.S. Received several distinguished corporate performance awards including:

- Award For Above And Beyond The Call Of Duty (1996)
- TQM Team of the Quarter (1993 and 1994)
- Consumer Affairs Award for Continued Excellent Performance (1990 and 1992)
- Consumer Affairs Award of Excellence (1986 and 1989)

Operations Manager — Customer Response Information Services (1993 to Present)

One of only three professionals retained by the company following complete downsizing of the
in-house customer response organization and start-up of outsourced operation. Retained
responsibilities as Operations Manager (since 1989) while shifting focus to a nine-site organization (two large contracted centers and seven remote, in-house centers).

Currently direct a team of 150 vendor-based contractors and 15 managers nationwide handling
over 2.5 million calls annually. Manage an $8 million annual operating budget. Negotiate
vendor contracts and monitor vendor compliance with operating standard and objectives (e.g.,
call volume, call duration, productivity, documentation, customer satisfaction).

- Led the successful transition from in-house to outsourced operation. Met 100% of all target
  dates and milestones. New operation has reduced cost per contact by 25% in two years with
  long-term projections indicating further reductions in both call and mail response costs.

- Wrote a complete business plan to standardize all policies and procedures (e.g., coupon
  refunds, claims processing, nutritional information, shipping) and provide contractors with
  a single operational reference manual.

- Designed/directed a 13,000 hour training program at vendor site. Educated personnel in
  Simpson standards, quality objectives, customer satisfaction and 3000+ products.

Operations Manager — Customer Response Information Center (1989 to 1993)

Promoted to direct the start-up and management of an integrated, full-service customer response and fulfillment center. Established strategic plans and operating goals, designed departmental infrastructure, determined staffing and technology requirements, and created policies/procedures for all facets of service management. Administered a $4.8 million budget and directed a staff of 80. Managed crisis communications and national product recalls.

- Built internal customer response organization from ground floor into a nationwide operation servicing more than one million customers annually.

- Transitioned customer response from a function that had been scattered throughout the corporation into a cohesive and accountable work group. Reduced costs per contract by 60% and mail turnaround time from 21+ days to three.

- Wrote business plan and led introduction of voice response technology. Co-directed project from initial feasibility/cost analysis through vendor sourcing and final implementation.

- Devised an employee hotline to obtain recommendations for productivity and quality improvements. Reduced operating costs by more than $500,000.

- Led internal training programs to enhance staff capabilities (e.g., communications, customer management, problem resolution, documentation). Created a forum for the ongoing exchange of information between all core operating functions.

Working in cooperation with executive management team, developed reengineering strategy to transition to outsourced consumer response operations. Effectively directed the complete downsizing of internal department and accepted new assignment directing the contracted response operation.

Customer Information Analyst (1987 to 1989)

Direct liaison between the Customer Response Information Center and Marketing, Quality Assurance, Legal and Manufacturing. Translated information regarding consumer issues, trends and market opportunities to support diverse product development, design, packaging, distribution and promotional efforts. Conducted detailed analyses of consumer data, identified and research complaints and resolved issues impacting consumer purchasing/satisfaction.

Senior Home Economist / Chef (1985 to 1987)
Development Technologist (1984 to 1985)

Promoted within six months to product development position providing critical technical, culinary and consumer expertise to lead expansion of Simpson's product portfolio.

EDUCATION: **MBA**, Ohio State University, 1985
               MS, Institutional Management, University of Illinois, 1983
               BS, Food & Nutrition, Florida A&M University, 1981

PROFESSIONAL ACTIVITIES:

Member   Society of Consumer Affairs Professionals, Incoming Call Center Management
Presenter   "Training & Hiring", Customer Service Organization National Conference, 1993

ENGINEERING

Positions

Associate Engineer

Chemical Engineer

Chief Engineer

Chief Scientist

Design Engineer

Development Engineer

Director of Engineering

Director of Quality Assurance

Director of R&D

Electrical Engineer

Electronic Engineer

Engineering Associate

Engineering Manager

Environmental Engineer

Facilities Engineer

Hardware Engineer

Industrial Engineer

Laboratory Manager

Laboratory Researcher

Lead Engineer

Maintenance Engineer

Manufacturing Engineer

Mechanical Engineer

Nuclear Engineer

Optics Engineer

Plant Engineer

Process Engineer
Professional Engineer
Project Director
Project Engineer
Project Manager
Quality Engineer
Quality Manager
R&D Engineer
Research Specialist
Scientist
Senior Engineer
Senior Project Manager
Software Engineer
Systems Engineer
Team Leader
Test Engineer
Vice President of Development
Vice President of Engineering
Vice President of Technical Operations
Vice President of Technical Services

KeyWords

Benchmark - **Benchmarked** best practices for systems, electronics and communications engineering.

Capital Project - Managed $4 million **capital project** for the development of facilities engineering, renovation and new construction projects.

Chemical Engineering - Advanced **chemical engineering** processes through introduction of leading edge prototyping, testing and quality management protocols.

Commissioning - Directed **commissioning** of over $10 million in new industrial facilities.

Computer-Aided Design (CAD) - Outsourced **CAD** engineering to better utilize resources of internal staff for advanced systems design.

Computer-Aided Engineering (CAE) - Introduced **CAE** methodologies into GE's in-house R&D department.

Computer-Aided Manufacturing (CAM) - Delivered a 22% gain in production yields following implementation of **CAM** processes.

Cross-Functional Team - Led a 200-person **cross-functional team** challenged to enhance systems performance through improved engineering capabilities.

Customer Management - Coordinated headquarters and field engineering personnel responsible for **customer management**, loyalty and retention.

Development Engineering - Managed a $4 million budget for **development engineering** and prototype design projects.

Efficiency - Delivered a 23% gain in departmental **efficiency** through introduction of advanced engineering, technical support and documentation procedures.

Electrical Engineering - Selected from a competitive group of more than 200 candidates for admission to USC's **Electrical Engineering** School.

Electronics Engineering - Graduated #1 in class of 420 with a M.S. Degree in **Electronics Engineering**.

Engineering Change Order (ECO) - Issued **ECOs** as mandated by U.S. Department of Energy for $12 million systems development project.

Engineering Documentation - Standardized **engineering documentation** and facilitated an immediate increase in field productivity.

Environmental Engineering - Recruited by CEO to direct the start-up and subsequent management of Dow's first in-house **Environmental Engineering** Department.

Ergonomic Techniques - Pioneered advanced **ergonomic techniques**, reduced employee absences 40%+ and lowered workers' compensation costs $2+ million annually.

Experimental Design - Accelerated **experimental design** with the recruitment of two Ph.D. scientists.

Experimental Methods - Redesigned **experimental methods** to eliminate non-essential tasks and expedite project completion.

Facilities Engineering - Managed a 32-person, $15 million **Facilities Engineering** Department responsible for 18 manufacturing, distribution and public warehousing sites.

Fault Analysis - Introduced advanced **fault analysis** and isolation procedures that increased systems availability by 45%.

Field Performance - Measured **field performance** based on systems operability and user functionality.

Final Customer Acceptance - Managed **final customer acceptance** and systems testing for all new technology installations.

Hardware Engineering - Directed **hardware engineering** and testing for new systems deployment.

Industrial Engineering - Created the corporation's first-ever **Industrial Engineering** Department to enhance ergonomic design of manufacturing and distribution facilities.

Industrial Hygiene - Trained staff responsible for field training and information dissemination regarding **industrial hygiene** and safety requirements.

Maintenance Engineering - Managed 100-person department responsible for **maintenance engineering** and systems documentation at Xerox's flagship manufacturing plant.

Manufacturing Engineering - Senior Executive leading a 200-person **manufacturing engineering** group supporting facilities throughout North America, Latin America, Europe and the Pacific Rim.

Manufacturing Integration - Facilitated **manufacturing integration** of newly-acquired technology resources.

Methods Design - Supervised **methods design** for chemical, mechanical, HVAC and electronics engineering.

Mechanical Engineering - Delivered over $20 million in **mechanical engineering** projects on time and within budget despite difficult field conditions.

Nuclear Engineering - Challenged to revitalize the corporation's **Nuclear Engineering** Division and facilitate development/delivery of new product and systems technology.

Occupational Safety & Health Administration (OSHA) - Administered the corporation's **OSHA** compliance and training program.

Operating & Maintenance (O&M) - Authored **O&M** manuals for all facilities.

Optics Engineering - Innovated advanced **optics engineering** methods and processes to accelerate product development and global market launch.

Plant Engineering - Managed a 45-person **plant engineering** team responsible for new facilities construction and large-scale renovation.

Process Development - Re-invented the corporation's **process development** programs to link engineering with operations and support long-term performance/productivity gains.

Process Engineering - Led team responsible for **process engineering**, design and implementation.

Process Standardization - Orchestrated **process standardization** of all activities involving electrical and electronics engineering teams.

Product Design - Credited with **product design** of advanced chemical compounds critical to continued AIDS research and protocol development.

Product Development Cycle - Directed a two-year **product development cycle** for the introduction of advanced navigation systems and technologies.

Product Functionality - Challenged to enhance **product functionality** with the introduction of new electronics technologies.

Product Innovation - Guided **product innovation** across multiple engineering disciplines, contributing to a better than 45% gain in sales, profits and market share ratings.

Product Lifecycle Management - Chaired in-house committee responsible for **product lifecycle management**, from initial design and engineering through commercialization.

Product Manufacturability - Enhanced **product manufacturability** with the introduction of an in-house systems engineering and design group.

Product Reliability - Enhanced **product reliability** to the strongest in the electronics industry with the introduction of scheduled preventive maintenance and testing programs.

Productivity Improvement - Delivered 34% **productivity improvement** following implementation of advanced robotics technology into large-scale manufacturing operations.

Project Costing - Guided **project costing** for all major R&D and engineering projects to ensure optimum profit margins and protect company assets.

Project Planning - Orchestrated interdisciplinary team responsible for **project planning**, scheduling, budgeting, costing and staffing.

Project Management - Senior Executive responsible for all field **project management** programs incorporating latest electronics and avionics technologies.

Prototype - Spearheaded **prototype** development of next generation products.

Quality Assurance - Created and managed a comprehensive **quality assurance**, quality review and regulatory compliance function.

Quality Engineering - Promoted as first-ever **quality engineering** professional in the entire Ericsson organization.

Regulatory Compliance - Achieved/surpassed all **regulatory compliance** standards despite issues negatively impacting product performance.

Research & Development (R&D) - Led a 12-person **R&D** team challenged to advance systems technologies into emerging new media markets.

Resource Management - Directed **resource management** function for all R&D facilities, technologies and data center operations worldwide.

Root Cause - Identified and eliminated **root cause** of non-performing electronic and electrical systems.

Scale-Up - Managed plant **scale-up** operations for all newly-commissioned environmental engineering and remediation facilities.

Software Engineering - Led 15-person **software engineering** team credited with the development and profitable commercialization of next generation product line.

Specifications - Authored **specifications** for all facilities development, technology development and manufacturing operations.

Statistical Analysis - Developed **statistical analysis** models to monitor field performance of advanced navigation systems.

Systems Engineering - Launched **systems engineering** group to managed predictive failure analysis, root cause analysis and remediation projects.

Systems Integration - Forged partnership with major hardware vendor to pioneer industry-leading **systems integration** projects.

Technical Briefings - Led **technical briefings** to state and federal government agency officials regarding the progress of the $45 million Des Moines Incineration Facility.

Technical Liaison Affairs - Managed **technical liaison affairs** between the corporation, vendors, customers and business partners worldwide.

Technology Development - Recognized for unprecedented performance in the leadership of advanced **technology development** programs.

Test Engineering - Revitalized **test engineering** operations and improved systems reliability by 19%.

Turnkey - Planned, staffed and directed field operations for over $200 million in **turnkey** design and engineering projects.

Work Methods Analysis - Conducted large-scale **work method analysis** project to identify strategies to enhance productivity, quality and performance.

WALTER N. BUSEY

9340 Balmont Avenue   Home   (615) 321-6547
Mesa, Arizona 86333   Office (615) 987-2312

DESIGN, ENGINEERING & MANUFACTURING
Advanced Information, Telecommunications, Electronic Packaging Technologies
Expertise in Team Building, Productivity/Efficiency Gain, Quality & Resource Maximization

CORE COMPETENCIES:

- Product Design & Mechanical Engineering
- Project Planning & Management
- Environmental Testing
- Reliability & Performance Analysis
- Automated Design Technologies
- Concurrent Design & Engineering

- Production & Assembly Operations
- Product Cost & Production Scheduling
- Subcontractor Negotiations
- Materials Planning & Management
- Product Testing & Prototyping
- Customer Presentations & Negotiations

PROFESSIONAL EXPERIENCE:

Engineering Manager (Section Supervisor)   1988 to Present
Space Inc., Mesa, Arizona

Senior Engineering Manager with full responsibility for strategic planning, staffing, budgeting and technical performance of all power control electronic system design projects. Lead team of 15 professional engineers throughout entire project cycle, from initial design through prototype, test, quality and transition to full-scale production.

- Manage $4 million in annual project budgets. Completed 10+ projects over eight years with total cost of over $30 million.
- Coordinate production planning and scheduling, purchasing and subcontracting. Provide engineering expertise to internal and outsourced manufacturing teams involved in supply/material management programs.
- Lead technical presentations to major customers nationwide for both new contracts and renewals. Instrumental in winning over $1.2 billion in contract awards.
- Spearhead project teams responsible for the redesign and improved manufacturability of existing products and technologies.
- Coordinate the selection and integration of advanced technologies for project design, vibration and thermal analysis, scheduling, systems integration and other core functions.

RESULTS:

- Built a talented and technically proficient mechanical engineering team successful in delivering cost-effective, high-performance designs, products and technologies.
- Spearheaded the redesign of assembly processes for a major systems component and delivered $500,000 in annual cost savings.
- Implemented custom hybrid circuits/surface mount components, reducing volume 70%.
- Directed team in the standardization and documentation of all mechanical engineering processes and methods for electronic box design.

Engineering Manager   1985 to 1988
Greinert Systems, Palo Alto, California

Recruited back to previous employer as Manager of Mast Engineering, a sophisticated mechanical engineering group designing mobile, collapsible antenna systems for deployment worldwide. Transferred to Mechanical Design Project Manager on a multi-million dollar project. Responsible for managing cost, schedule and technical performance of reconfigured rack-mounted ESM equipment. Led a team of seven professional engineers and up to $1 million in annual project budgets.

- Appointed to design team facilitating the concept development of electronic support measures equipment for unique customer applications.
- Actively involved in the implementation of an advanced noise testing simulation facility.

Engineering Specialist   1981 to 1985
Litton-Applied Technology, Sunnyvale, California

Lead Engineer for more than $250,000 annually in systems design projects, ranging from computer components to advanced digital and RF electronics. Concurrent responsibility for the design evaluation and oversight of power supply and microwave device subcontractors.

- Facilitated the selection, acquisition and integration of workstation technology into the Mechanical Engineering Group to enhance finite element analysis capabilities.

Senior Engineer   1977 to 1981
Greinert Systems, Needham, Massachusetts

Only mechanical engineer in the entire design facility. Produced mechanical and environmentally resistant designs for sophisticated, high-vibration applications. Assisted in project budgeting, scheduling, task definition and team supervision/technical support.

- Appointed Cost Proposal Manager for large RFP.
- Doubled yield of high voltage magnetics in production through product/process redesign.

EDUCATION:

M.S., Engineering Management, University of California - Los Angeles, 1991
M.S., Mechanical Engineering, University of California - Santa Cruz, 1986
B.S., Mechanical Engineering, *Magna Cum Laude*, Boston University, 1977

PERSONAL PROFILE:

Two-year tour of duty with the U.S. Army. Vietnam Era Veteran. Honorably discharged.
Design and assemble personalized golf clubs as a small, independent venture.
NCGA Golf Tournament Player. Member of Arizona Golf Association.

FINANCE, ACCOUNTING & AUDITING

Positions

Accounting Manager
Assistant Director
Audit Manager
Certified Financial Planner (CFP)
Certified Public Accountant (CPA)
Chief Administrative Officer (CAO)
Chief Financial Officer (CFO)
Chief Operating Officer (COO)
Comptroller
Controller
Deputy Director
Director of Corporate Tax
Director of Finance
Finance Manager
General Manager
Group Manager
Senior Accountant
Senior Auditor
Staff Accountant
Staff Auditor
Tax Director
Treasurer
Vice President of Corporate Development
Vice President of Finance
Vice President of Finance & Administration

KeyWords

Accounts Payable - Streamlined **accounts payable** functions, established common vendor files, eliminated duplication and reduced monthly processing time by 20%.

Accounts Receivable - Introduced improved **accounts receivable** and collection policies that decreased outstanding receivables by an average of 40% monthly.

Asset Disposition - Determined proper **asset disposition**, sale and leasing options following plant divestiture.

Asset Management - Established **Asset Management** Division to control $55 million in capital equipment and technology.

Asset Purchase - Structured and executed **asset purchase** of Zylog Corporation in Canada.

Audit Controls - Implemented a stringent program of **audit controls** to reverse previous findings during Coopers & Lybrand external audit review.

Audit Management - Directed financial and operational **audit management** programs of 89 sales, manufacturing and distribution businesses worldwide.

Capital Budgets - Formulated, justified and managed $8 million in **capital budgets** annually.

Cash Management - Redesigned **cash management** processes, renegotiated banking relationships and created the corporation's first comprehensive corporate treasury function.

Commercial Paper - Structured and negotiated over $125 million in **commercial paper** transactions with Chase Manhattan Bank.

Corporate Development - Provided strategic, financial, legal and negotiations expertise for **corporate development** initiatives, including mergers, acquisitions, joint ventures and technology licenses.

Corporate Tax - Led a team of eight responsible for **corporate tax** filings in more than 1000 local, state and federal jurisdictions.

Cost Accounting - Implemented automated **cost accounting** systems to analyze all labor, material, technology, process, quality, testing and manufacturing costs for each product line.

Cost Avoidance - Introduced proactive management techniques to strengthen focus on **cost avoidance** and elimination within each manufacturing process.

Cost Reduction - Delivered over $2.8 million in first year labor, inventory and delivery **cost reductions**.

Cost/Benefit Analysis - Conducted large-scale **cost/benefit analysis** studies to capitalize upon long-term growth and profit improvement opportunities.

Credit & Collections - Reduced DSO by 28% through improved **credit and collection** processes.

Debt Financing - Negotiated $2.5 million in **debt financing** with a major banking institution and a regionally-based venture capital firm.

Divestiture - Planned and executed profitable **divestiture** of the $1.5 million emerging electronic commerce product line.

Due Diligence - Orchestrated complex **due diligence** reviews in cooperation with outside financial advisors, accountants and legal counsel.

Employee Stock Ownership Plan (ESOP) - Led Weinhold Winers through successful LBO and **ESOP** transactions, creating a corporation that is now ranked #1 in nationwide market share.

Equity Financing - Structured a three-way partnership between 3M, Telecom and IBM for $160 million in **equity financing** for new technology venture.

Feasibility Analysis - Led 22-person finance team managing complex **feasibility analysis** and developing projections for TLC's global market expansion.

Financial Analysis - Created team-based **financial analysis** models integrating financial data for all 52 operating locations worldwide.

Financial Audits - Planned and managed more than 50 **financial audits** throughout all Xerox sales and service operations.

Financial Controls - Designed and implemented a comprehensive program of **financial controls** and accountability to reverse previous years' losses.

Financial Models - Developed **financial models** for cost/benefit analysis, joint venture analysis, staffing analysis and compensation design.

Financial Planning - Directed **financial planning** functions for both U.S. and European operations, and presented final results to the Board of Directors.

Financial Reporting - Eliminated unnecessary **financial reporting** and created a comprehensive PC-based program to integrate financial data from all operating divisions.

Foreign Exchange (FX) - Implemented **foreign exchange** and currency hedging programs to protect IBM's Asian assets.

Initial Public Offering (IPO) - Raised $54 million in public and private investment to fund **IPO**.

Internal Controls - Designed and implemented a comprehensive program of **internal controls** governing finance, accounting, capital assets and technology acquisitions.

International Finance - Resigned core domestic financial systems and processes to create a new **international finance** function to support business expansion and product line diversification.

Investment Management - Assigned concurrent executive responsibility for administration of $50 million in **investment management**.

Investor Accounting - Personally managed **investor accounting**, reporting and presentations.

Investor Relations - Created a sophisticated **investor relations** programs, restoring credibility throughout the financial community.

Job Costing - Restructured **job costing** standards to eliminate excess expenses and strengthen bottom-line profitability of all key projects.

Letters of Credit - Issued $10 million in **letters of credit** to fund the acquisition of gold, silver and other precious commodities.

Leveraged Buy-Out (LBO) - Led management team in successful **LBO** of ABC Transportation, formed new executive team and re-launched national sales programs.

Liability Management - Created a formal **liability management** program to control major losses resulting from downward trend in the aerospace industry.

Make/Buy Analysis - Designed PC-based templates to support **make/buy analysis** for the Construction and Real Estate Investment divisions.

Margin Improvement - Restructured corporate pricing on all major product lines and delivered a 12% **margin improvement**.

Merger - Identified opportunity, negotiated and executed transaction for the 1999 Xerox and IBM **merger**.

Operating Budgets - Managed $2 million in annual **operating budgets** allocated for personnel, facilities and administrative expenses.

Operational Audits - Planned and directed **operational audits** of all Red Cross blood banking facilities to ensure compliance with Red Cross policy and federal regulations.

Partnership Accounting - Designed multi-tiered **partnership accounting** systems for 25 limited and general partnership real estate development projects.

Profit/Loss (P&L) Analysis - Reviewed historical data to prepare complex **P&L analysis** as part of acquisition due diligence plan.

Profit Gains - Accelerated **profit gains** through an aggressive program of facilities consolidation, staff reduction and asset divestiture.

Project Accounting - Managed **project accounting** function for the $3.6 million Bayside Tunnel Development Project in New Orleans.

Project Financing - Negotiated $2.5 million in World Bank **project financing** for economic development programs in Ghana.

Regulatory Compliance Auditing - Established a structured process to expedite **regulatory compliance auditing**, reporting and defense.

Return on Assets (ROA) - Increased **ROA** on real estate investments by 26%.

Return on Equity (ROE) - Invested $10 million in start-up industrial products company and, over six years, achieved an average 22% **ROE**.

Return on Investment (ROI) - Purchased failing company, revitalized sales and distribution, and delivered a 48% **ROI** to investor group.

Revenue Gain - Negotiated distribution contracts throughout the Pacific Rim, delivering a 12% **revenue gain** in first year.

Risk Management - Strategized and implemented TouchTone's first-ever corporate **risk management**, insurance and pension plan administration function.

Shareholder Relations - Restored corporate credibility through a combined **shareholder relations** and shareholder communications initiative.

Stock Purchase - Identified opportunity for market expansion and negotiated transaction for $837 million **stock purchase** of the Telephone Group, Inc.

Strategic Planning - Facilitated cross-functional executive team through a complex, multi-year **strategic planning** process.

Treasury - Redefined the vision, mission and objectives of the Corporate **Treasury** Department to align financial targets with operational goals.

Trust Accounting - Developed and implemented formal **trust accounting** and pension plan reporting functions to replace reliance on third party administrator.

Workpapers - Streamlined accounting processes to reduce **workpaper** and documentation requirements.

David M. Williams, CMA

23564 Mountain View Court
Portland, Oregon 98326
(503) 335-9832

SENIOR OPERATING & FINANCE EXECUTIVE

Corporate Planning / Financial Analysis / Financial Reporting / Treasury / Credit Management
Mergers & Acquisitions / Joint Ventures / Strategic Marketing Partnerships / Creative Leadership

Top-flight professional career as a member of the senior management team of several high-growth, high-tech corporations. Contributed millions of dollars in revenues and profits through achievements in debt and equity management, operating cost reduction, market development, contract negotiations and general business management.

1982	**Certified Management Accountant (CMA)**
1979	**MBA**, University of Washington
1976	**BS / Business & Finance**, Seattle Pacific University

PROFESSIONAL EXPERIENCE:

Principal   1995 to Present
FINANCIAL SERVICES NETWORK, Portland, Oregon

Founded executive consulting practice specializing in strategic business planning, finance, investment acquisition, marketing, technology development and organizational change. Major projects:

Acting CFO with Greene Video (media post production company) to represent their interests in their complex and high-profile acquisition by MultiMedia Company (multimedia entertainment group which had just completed $50+ million IPO). Introduced the parties and negotiated key elements of acquisition agreement between owners, attorneys and financial counsel. Devoted nine months to managing an aggressive financial and operations reorganization prior to acquisition.

- Restored credibility throughout the banking, credit and vendor communities.
- Restructured over $8 million in corporate debt as part of buyout by MultiMedia Company.
- Negotiated and resolved complex IRS issues, saving over $300,000 in principal and penalty liabilities.

Senior Finance & Marketing Manager, U.S. Capital, a premier provider of capital equipment acquisition and leasing services and business partner of my previous employer. Retained to launch the start-up of sales, marketing and business development programs throughout the Western U.S.

- Delivered significant financial contracts and sales transactions. Closed $5 million in less than one year.
- Structured, negotiated and closed leasing transactions between technology providers (e.g., Philips Symons, Sony, Discreet Logic) and financial institutions.

Director of Finance & Administration   1992 to 1995
SYMONS TELEVISION SYSTEMS, INC., San Francisco, California
($100 million manufacturer of electronic broadcast equipment for networks and cable systems worldwide.)

Recruited as **Manager of Credit & Financial Services** for the corporation's marketing, sales and field service organization supporting operations in North America, South America and the Pacific Rim. Promoted to **Director of Finance & Administration** for the group within first year and given full responsibility for Accounting, MIS, Sales Administration, Human Resources and Operations (e.g., logistics, inventory, shipping, purchasing). Staff accountability for 20 professional and support personnel.

SYMONS TELEVISION SYSTEMS, INC. *(Continued):*

- Established new operating division to fund customer acquisitions. Negotiated strategic partnerships with lending institution and third party agent for funding, finance administration and collection. Business unit has now grown to $44 million in annual sales revenues.

- Rewrote corporate credit policy, centralized collections on a regional basis and improved receivables by 20 days. Consulted with corporate legal staff in Venezuela to develop strategic and tactical plans for recovery of $1+ million in past due receivables.

Chief Financial Officer / Executive Vice President   1987 to 1992
LINTEK, INC., Cadwell, Oregon
(High-growth manufacturer of high-tech underwater electrical systems.)

Senior Finance Executive directing corporate finance, accounting, credit, treasury, tax, shareholder relations, venture capital negotiations and lease/contract negotiations. Concurrent executive management responsibility for business development, marketing and operations.

- Restructured corporate debt and increased company net worth by more than 100%.
- Negotiated financial, legal and contractual terms for 10-year international license with U.K. company for technology marketing and distribution. Generated immediate cash and market share.
- Featured in Wall Street Journal Network Business News Small Business Report for negotiation of export financing from the State of California and EXIM Bank to fund Lintek's international business operations. Repaid $1+ million in funds within two years.
- Led aggressive U.S. and foreign patent acquisition program to protect product design and applications under development.

Chief Operating Officer / Executive Vice President / Board Director   1982 to 1987
MOUNTAIN REGIONAL BANK, North Peak, California

Senior Operating Executive leading an aggressive reorganization and restructuring of multi-branch banking system to position company for sale. Directed a staff of 90 in corporate finance and administration, legal, accounting, budgeting, human resources, sales/marketing, banking services, lending/credit, customer service and regulatory affairs.

- Reengineered all core business processes throughout the organization. Achieved long-term improvements in cost savings, profitability and productivity.
- Delivered 25%+ average rate of return on commercial properties.
- Successfully penetrated new market niches and expanded professional clientele.

Administration & Corporate Planning Executive   1979 to 1982
COASTAL BANK, Los Angeles, California

PROFESSIONAL ACTIVITIES:

Teaching	Guest Lecturer in Finance, Washington State University
	Guest Lecturer in Finance, Certified Management Accountants Workshop
Affiliations	Broadcast Cable Financial Managers Association (Chair, Membership Committee)
Honors/Awards	Outstanding Young Men of American Award, United States Jaycees, 1981 and 1984
	Toastmaster of the Year (local chapter), Toastmasters International, 1974

GENERAL MANAGEMENT, SENIOR MANAGEMENT & CONSULTING

Positions

Acting Director
Acting President
Acting Vice President
Assistant Vice President
Associate Director
Board Director
Business Manager
Business Unit Leader
Chairperson/Chairman
Chief Administrative Officer (CAO)
Chief Executive Officer (CEO)
Chief Operating Officer (COO)
Consultant
Corporate Director
Corporate Vice President
Director
Division Director
Division Vice President
Executive Consultant
Executive Director
Executive Vice President (EVP)
First Vice President
Founder

General Manager

General Partner

Interim Director

Interim Executive

Interim President

Interim Vice President

Management Consultant

Manager

Managing Director

Managing Partner

Officer

Operations Manager

Owner

Partner

President

Principal

Second Vice President

Senior Manager

Senior Vice President

Superintendent

Vice President

KeyWords

Accelerated Growth - Led RDL through a period of **accelerated growth** and international market expansion, resulting in a 200% gain in revenues and 300% improvement in EBIT.

Acting Executive - Appointed **Acting Executive** with full responsibility for strategic planning and business leadership during year-long nation-wide search for new CEO.

Advanced Technology - Pioneered the design, development and market launch of **advanced technology** for both information and telecommunications applications.

Benchmarking - Led **benchmarking** project to develop best-in-class manufacturing practices.

Business Development - Guided marketing and **business development** programs throughout the U.S., Canada, Latin America and Europe.

Business Reengineering - Spearheaded the most successful **business reengineering** project in IBM's history, delivering a 25% reduction in annual operating costs while driving revenue improvement by more than 50% across all major product categories.

Capital Projects - Directed over $18 million in **capital projects** and technology acquisitions to upgrade manufacturing complex.

Competitive Market Position - Conducted worldwide competitor intelligence surveys to determine Smith's most aggressive **competitive market position** for long-term revenue and profit growth.

Consensus Building - Demonstrated proficiency in **consensus building**, team building and executive liaison affairs.

Continuous Process Improvement - Pioneered innovative technologies and work systems to drive **continuous process improvement** across all four manufacturing and distribution facilities.

Corporate Administration - Appointed to the Board of Directors with responsibility for all **corporate administration**, recordkeeping and stockholder reporting functions.

Corporate Communications - Expanded **corporate communications** programs to include monthly direct response campaigns to the top 250 customers nationwide.

Corporate Culture Change - Credited as the Lead Executive directing IBM's successful **corporate culture change** throughout all 300+ strategic business units worldwide.

Corporate Development - Personally structured, negotiated and executed 25 mergers, acquisitions, joint ventures, strategic alliances, technology licenses and other **corporate development** projects with business partners worldwide.

Corporate Image - Created a new, high-impact **corporate image** introduced through major print and broadcast media channels nationwide.

Corporate Legal Affairs - Recruited to revitalize **corporate legal affairs** and introduce improved strategies to protect corporate intelligence, technologies and markets.

Corporate Mission - Defined **corporate mission** in response to rapidly changing market demographics.

Corporate Vision - Created a common **corporate vision** across all major product lines and strategic business units.

Cost Avoidance - Introduced best practice work processes to extend the lifecycle of capital manufacturing equipment and promote **cost avoidance** over the next five years.

Cost Reduction - Pioneered innovative process improvements that **reduced costs** by $450,000 in first six months.

Crisis Communications - Directed high-profile **crisis communications** arising from major product recall.

Cross-Cultural Communications - Demonstrated proficiency in **cross-cultural communications** with business partners throughout the Pacific Rim and Far East regions.

Cross-Functional Team Leadership - Selected by the CEO to direct a **cross-functional team** evaluating potential reengineering, change management and technology acquisitions.

Customer Loyalty - Recognized as a pioneer in **customer loyalty** and retention within the highly-competitive consumer products industry.

Customer Retention - Introduced interim customer communications programs, a series of special promotions and a one-on-one service program that improved **customer retention** rates by 78%.

Customer-Driven Management - Challenged to refocus organization and introduce a **customer-driven management** philosophy to regain competitive lead.

Decision-Making Authority - Held full **decision-making authority** for all expenditures for the Aerospace & Engineering Divisions of QDL.

Efficiency Improvement - Drove an organization-wide **efficiency improvement** project, integrated similar functions into core operations and reduced costs by 12% in first year.

Emerging Business Venture - Identified opportunity, structured partnership and captured **emerging business ventures** throughout Eastern Europe.

Entrepreneurial Leadership - Provided decisive, action-driven, **entrepreneurial leadership**.

European Economic Community (EEC) - Guided corporate expansion throughout emerging and mature markets within the **EEC**.

Executive Management - Member of 6-person **Executive Management** Team credited with transitioning Apex from multi-year losses to sustained profitability.

Executive Presentations - Designed and led **executive presentations** to Board of Directors, shareholders, Wall Street analysts and financial auditors.

Financial Management - Member of 6-person Senior Management Team and the most Senior Financial Executive responsible for all financial planning, **financial management** and long-range business development functions.

Financial Restructuring - Orchestrated an aggressive **financial restructuring** of all technology support operations, reducing annual costs by $2.8 million and strengthening competitive lead.

Global Market Expansion - Guided Johnson Controls' expansion throughout the **global market**.

High-Growth Organization - Delivered strong revenue and profit results in start-up, turnaround and **high-growth organizations**.

Infrastructure - Redesigned and streamlined organizational **infrastructure** to capitalize upon human resource, operational and financial competencies.

Interim Executive - Appointed **Interim Executive** with full P&L responsibility for $8 million corporation.

Leadership Development - Designed **leadership development** programs for all mid-level and senior management personnel throughout the organization.

Long-Range Planning - Guided **long-range planning** for operations, sales, marketing and customer service.

Management Development - Introduced leadership training, technology training, communication skills training and other **management development** programs.

Margin Improvement - Realigned product mix and captured a 12% **margin improvement**.

Market Development - Identified opportunity to expand customer reach and led targeted **market development** programs throughout Central and South America.

Market-Driven Management - Revitalized corporation and introduced **market-driven management** systems to accelerate revenue growth against competition.

Marketing Management - Senior Executive leading strategic planning, product development and **marketing management** programs across all seven major business units.

Matrix Management - Operated within a **matrix management** environment transcending all core business, operating, financial, marketing and human resource functions.

Multi-Function Experience - Promoted rapidly through a series of increasingly responsible management positions, gaining broad-based, **multi-function experience** across corporate finance, marketing, strategic planning and product management.

Multi-Industry Experience - Gained broad **multi-industry experience** within the plastics, metals and ceramics manufacturing industries.

Multi-Site Operations Management - Senior Executive with full P&L responsibility for **multi-site operations management** of production facilities in Frankfurt, Rome and Salzburg.

New Business Development - Challenged to identify and capture opportunities for **new business development**, market growth and revenue improvement throughout the Northeastern U.S.

Operating Infrastructure - Streamlined corporate **operating infrastructure**, consolidated administrative functions from six offices into headquarters, replaced non-performing staff and introduced a performance incentive program.

Operating Leadership - Provided decisive, proactive and market-driven **operating leadership** within a politically volatile business market.

Organization(al) Culture - Redefined corporate vision, rewrote mission statement and revitalized **organizational culture**.

Organization(al) Development - Pioneered innovative **organizational development** initiatives including pay for performance, diversity management, process redesign and change management.

Participative Management - Fostered employee empowerment and **participative management** practices throughout the manufacturing organization.

Policy Development - Directed **policy development** for all sales, service and support functions nationwide.

Performance Improvement - Led 6-person task force in the design and implementation of **performance improvement** initiatives throughout all 22 branch operations.

Proactive Leadership - Credited with providing the corporation with **proactive leadership** despite four changes in ownership over a two-year period.

Process Ownership - Introduced **process ownership** into the quality function, eliminating the need for physical inspection and improving product quality ratings to a consistent 98%.

Process Reengineering - Spearheaded **process reengineering** and redesign of all core production planning, scheduling and manufacturing management systems.

Productivity Improvement - Delivered measurable **productivity improvements** across the field organization.

Profit & Loss (P&L) Management - Promoted to General Manager with full operating and **P&L management** responsibility for $8.2 million distribution facility.

Profit Growth - Implemented new selling strategies designed to accelerate **profit growth** and expansion into high-growth mass merchant markets.

Project Management - Appointed Leader of 22-person **project management** team leading technology introductions and enhancements throughout RDL's nationwide logistics organization.

Quality Improvement - Recruited to provide strategic and tactical leadership for quality improvement and **quality management** functions.

Relationship Management - Directed key account **relationship management** functions for 25 of the corporation's largest customer accounts.

Reengineering - Led corporate-wide **reengineering** and revitalization program, reducing losses by $2.8 million and improving market share ratings by 29%.

Reorganization - Challenged to lead the corporation through an aggressive **reorganization** and divestiture of non-performing business units, products and technologies.

Return-On-Assets (ROA) - Restructured corporate assets and improved **ROA** by 36%.

Return-On-Equity (ROE) - Invested over $10 million in emerging technology ventures with goal of a better than 52% **ROE**.

Return-On-Investment (ROI) - Replaced in-house benefits professional with third-party administrator and improved **ROI** by 18% within first year.

Revenue Growth - Drove 27% **revenue growth** against stiff market competition in the New England region.

Sales Management - Led a 62-person, multinational **sales management** team supporting 1000+ distributors worldwide.

Service Design/Delivery - Delivered 22% improvement in customer retention through improved **service design/delivery** systems.

Signatory Authority - Held $2 million contract **signatory authority** for the corporation.

Start-Up Venture - Challenged to identify and capitalize upon opportunities to develop and direct **start-up ventures** in the former Soviet Union markets.

Strategic Development - Evaluated new product opportunities and directed **strategic development** of business plans, financial projections, marketing plans and field sales teams.

Strategic Partnership - Structured and negotiated a **strategic partnership** with Mobil Oil to manage joint exploration projects in the Middle East.

Tactical Planning/Leadership - Transitioned strategy into **tactical plans** to drive market growth and diversification.

Team Building - Introduced performance-driven **team building** processes into the materials management and engineering organizations.

Team Leadership - Provided decisive **team leadership** and direction to a 2000-person manufacturing organization.

Total Quality Management (TQM) - Championed the development and implementation of **TQM** programs and achieved ISO 9002 within six months.

Transition Management - Effectively guided Appollo Systems through six changes in operating executives and the resulting **transition management** functions.

Turnaround Management - Recognized by the Board of Directors for expertise in **turnaround management** and return to profitability of 3M's newest product marketing group.

World Class Organization - Transitioned NEBS from a family-owned start-up venture into a **world class manufacturing and service organization**.

EDWARD T. PATTERSON

3985 Dunhill Drive
San Ramon, California 90631

Residence:	(315) 359-7873	Business:	(315) 359-8742
Email:	ETP@aol.com	Fax:	(315) 359-2676

SENIOR OPERATING & MANAGEMENT EXECUTIVE

Senior Executive with a long and successful career building start-up, turnaround and high-growth organizations. Delivered strong and sustainable financial gains in challenging markets nationwide through decisive leadership, influence and action. MBA Degree. Expertise includes:

General Business & Operations Management

- Distinguished performance on the executive management teams of four corporations, providing strategic leadership, vision and tactical action to deliver improved financial, performance and profit results. Successful in identifying and capitalizing upon new business opportunities through integration of technical, personnel, financial and operating resources to dominate markets and drive long-term asset and revenue gains. Accomplished in customer relationship management and high-quality customer service.

Corporate Finance & Deal Making

- Ten years experience structuring and negotiating complex corporate financing transactions with Wall Street bankers and brokers, venture capital firms, private investors and others to fund new ventures, market expansion initiatives, new product and service offerings, and cash flow. Participated and/or led over $2 billion in total financial transactions throughout career. Expert in investor relations and investor reporting. Experienced Board Director.

Advanced Technology

- Spearheaded development of proposed investment in client/server technology to develop innovative applications for consumer financial services. Led year-long project feasibility analysis and nationwide market research/market survey, developed complex risk analysis process, and identified optimum strategies for technology development, documentation, prototyping and full-scale market launch.

Technical / Non-Technical Communications

- Bridged the gap between executives and technology development teams to ensure that projects were financially viable, technically appropriate, and capable of meeting long-term organizational, productivity and performance goals. Able to communicate highly-technical information to non-technical personnel.

Marketing Management

- Conceived, developed and executed top-producing marketing campaigns across diverse customer sectors nationwide. Delivered unprecedented performance results through innovation in campaign design, production and marketing leadership. Strong qualifications in new product development and launch.

Team Building & Organizational Leadership

- Track record of success in building and leading top-producing professional, technical, support and management teams meeting the challenges of start-up, turnaround and high-growth organizations. Extensive background in management training and development, organizational design, business process design, budgeting and project leadership.

EDWARD T. PATTERSON - Page Two

PROFESSIONAL EMPLOYMENT HISTORY

Director   1996 to 1997
Pioneer Financial Services, San Ramon, California

Directed high-profile technology feasibility project for development of client/server PC network. Project was initiated to enhance competitive position, increase cross-sell performance, reduce staffing requirements, and automate the entire credit decisioning and documentation process. Managed a complex cost/risk analysis to evaluate "buy versus build." Authored recommendations for development, beta testing and deployment.

President / Chief Executive Officer / Director   1993 to 1995
Lewis Federal Bank, F.S.B., Lewis, California

Senior Operating Executive with full P&L responsibility for the turnaround, internal reorganization and market repositioning of this $125 million corporation. Directed operations at eight facilities and with a total workforce of 150. Developed successful strategy to divest under- and non-performing assets, restructured liabilities, renegotiated funding, and increased market penetration in all sectors. Provided long-term vision and created multi-year action plan. Achieved/surpassed all turnaround objectives.

National Director of Marketing & Business Development   1990 to 1993
Federal Housing Authority, Washington, D.C.

Joined the senior management team to spearhead an aggressive market expansion to position Federal Housing Authority as a diversified financial services institution. Developed business strategies to diversify customer base, established internal business systems and processes to accommodate increased workload, and pioneered innovative marketing programs. Directed development of award-winning "Community Banks - Main Street to Wall Street."

Vice President - Capital Markets   1988 to 1989
Resources, Inc., Provo, Utah

Recruited to plan and orchestrate the start-up of a new business venture, building new business infrastructure, designing internal operating processes, implementing new technology and driving new venture to profitability. Transitioned concept into full-scale operation and developed $200 million senior LBO debt portfolio.

Credit Manager   1980 to 1988
Citicorp / Citibank, New York, New York

Fast-track promotion through a series of increasingly responsible management positions leading high-profile start-up ventures, marketing organizations and new business development initiatives nationwide. Delivered strong and sustainable performance results in each position through success in team building and leadership.

Active duty with U.S. Army (1970 to 1974). Retired as Lt. Colonel in U.S. Army Reserve in 1995.

EDUCATION

MBA (Banking & Finance), Golden Gate University, 1979
BA (Sociology), University of California, 1977

HEALTHCARE

Positions

Administrator

Assistant Administrator

Budget Director

Chief Executive Officer (CEO)

Chief Financial Officer (CFO)

Chief Nursing Officer (CNO)

Chief Operating Officer (COO)

Clinical Marketing Director

Clinical Services Director

Controller

Director of Administration

Director of Billing

Director of Finance

Director of Inservice Education

Director of Patient Accounting

Director of Reimbursement

Executive Director

Executive Vice President (EVP)

Finance Manager

General Manager

Health Care Administrator

Inpatient Services Director

Managed Care Director

Medical Affairs Director

Medical Director

Nursing Administrator

Nursing Director

Nursing Home Administrator

Outpatient Services Director

President

Quality Assurance Director

Senior Nursing Executive

Vice President

KeyWords

Acute Care Facility - Chief Executive Officer of a 434-bed **acute care facility**, six free-standing community clinics and a large healthcare research complex.

Ambulatory Care - Structured three-year contractual agreement with Ryder for the delivery of on-site **ambulatory care** services at corporate headquarters.

Assisted Living - Established the region's first-ever **assisted living** center within the Monticello Retirement Village.

Capital Giving Campaign - Spearheaded multimedia communications, advertising and direct mail programs for a successful $10 million **capital giving campaign**.

Case Management - Created a multi-discipline **case management** protocol for the evaluation, diagnosis and treatment planning of all incoming HIV-positive patients.

Certificate of Need (CON) - Authored **Certificate of Need** requesting $2 billion in funding for development of 1000-bed research facility.

Chronic Care Facility - Recruited to plan and direct the financial turn-around of a 250-bed **chronic care facility** with affiliated hospice.

Clinical Services - Restructured healthcare delivery procedures to expand **clinical services** throughout the metropolitan region.

Community Hospital - Led 2-year construction project for the development of a 500-bed **community hospital** targeted to indigenous populations throughout Central Arkansas.

Community Outreach - Won Board funding for the development and execution of an aggressive **community outreach** and healthcare education program.

Continuity of Care - Implemented processes to enhance the **continuity of care** among surgeons, attending physicians, nursing staff and administration.

Cost Center - Transitioned **cost center** into profit-producing venture with the introduction of corporate contracts for on-site health examinations.

Electronic Claims Processing - Introduced **electronic claims processing** into group medical practice and improved collections by 34% annually.

Employee Assistance Program (EAP) - Launched the start-up, staffing, budgeting and service delivery of Westinghouse's first-ever **EAP**.

Emergency Medical Systems (EMS) - Joined the start-up management team developing the University of Maryland **Emergency Medical Systems** organization.

Fee Billing - Streamlined documentation processes and accelerated **fee billing** for private pay and Medicare patients.

Full Time Equivalent (FTE) - Staffed new healthcare facility with 120 **FTEs** and 60 on-call nursing personnel.

Grant Administration - Full management responsibility for **grant administration** of more than $200 million in annual research funds from Carnegie Mellon University, USC and Brigham Young.

Healthcare Administrator - Senior **Healthcare Administrator** with full operating, staffing, clinical, technical and P&L responsibility for the entire healthcare complex.

Healthcare Delivery Systems - Devoted 10 years to the research and design of integrated **healthcare delivery systems**, models and protocols.

Health Maintenance Organization (HMO) - Led presentations and won support of Board of Directors for the start-up of a new **HMO** focused on comprehensive, preventive healthcare.

Home Healthcare - Managed a large **home healthcare** agency offering in-home respiratory, physical and chemotherapy services.

Hospital Foundation - Established DC General's not-for-profit **hospital foundation** to support long-range funding, facilities expansion and pioneering research.

Industrial Medicine - Recruited as Raytheon's first-ever in-house physician to guide the development of a complete **industrial medicine** and occupational medicine facility.

Inpatient Care - Expanded **inpatient care** programs to include 24-hour nursing services for acutely ill patients diagnosed with Legionnaire's Disease.

Long-Term Care - Negotiated partnership with the USC Medical Center to establish a new **long-term care** facility for communicable diseases.

Managed Care - Forged innovative **managed care** partnerships with leading healthcare providers and administrators throughout Detroit.

Management Service Organization (MSO) - Integrated best practices from HMO and PPO practices throughout the region to create a comprehensive **MSO** network.

Multi-Hospital Network - Structured and negotiated the integration of Los Angeles' six primary care facilities to create a **multi-hospital network** offering comprehensive acute and long-term hospice care.

Occupational Health - Introduced an **occupational health** program with required preventive healthcare teaching and reduced on-the-job accidents by 45% in first year.

Outpatient Care - Expanded service offerings in a large **outpatient care** facility and increased number of annual patient visits by 18%.

Patient Accounting - Restructured the hospital's **patient accounting** operations and accelerated collections to the best in the region.

Patient Relations - Designed print and video communications to strengthen **patient relations** and the credibility of newly-renovated, inner-city hospital complex.

Peer Review - Managed **peer review** issues resulting from alleged malpractice incidents.

Physician Credentialing - Established and administered **physician credentialing** program for all new doctors entering the MSO network.

Physician Relations - Developed a formal **physician relations** program to attract and retain renowned cardiologists to the practice.

Practice Management - Created innovative **practice management** models and methodologies to strengthen quality of care.

Preferred Provider Organization (PPO) - Forged relationships with leading healthcare specialists throughout the region to create a unique **PPO** network offering comprehensive diagnostic and clinical services.

Preventive Medicine - Advocated for establishment of a comprehensive **preventive medicine** program throughout all public school and daycare facilities in Denver.

Primary Care - Transitioned from specialty urologic practice into **primary care** in response to changing patient demographics.

Provider Relations - Partnered clinical services with marketing programs to create a unique **provider relations** and provider support program.

Public Health Administration - Revitalized West Virginia's **Public Health Administration** services and policy.

Quality of Care - Introduced **quality of care** standards, protocols and reporting requirements to meet JCAHO standards.

Regulatory Standards (JCAHO) - Resolved long-standing non-compliance issues and achieved 100% compliance with all regulatory standards mandated by **JCAHO** and state agencies.

Rehabilitation Services - Negotiated public and private funding for the start-up of **rehabilitation services** for paraplegics, quadriplegics and other long-term rehab patients.

Reimbursement Program - Managed a multi-million dollar third-party **reimbursement program**, implemented new collection procedures and recovered over $90,000 in outstanding receivables.

Risk Management - Authored a formal **risk management** policy for the entire medical facility, all affiliated healthcare clinics and the region's largest healthcare research facility.

Service Delivery - Improved **service delivery** through restaffing and implementation of stringent quality of care standards.

Skilled Nursing Facility - Held full P&L, operating, staffing, regulatory and clinical service delivery responsibility for a 180-bed **skilled nursing facility**.

Third Party Administrator - Introduced new patient filing and documentation processes to meet changing requirements of **third party administrator**.

Utilization Review - Designed and administered **utilization review**, peer review and other internal quality management processes.

Wellness Programs - Forged the development of corporate **wellness programs** impacting all 3000+ employees of the RayChem Corporation.

HOWARD M. JOHNSON, MPA

9863 Constable Road
Wilmington, Delaware 19832

Residence: 302-786-5439   Email: HJohn@mcimail.net   Fax: (302) 786-6935

HEALTH CARE INDUSTRY EXECUTIVE
Managed Care / Hospitals & Clinics / Multi-Site Facilities

Cross-functional management expertise in the strategic planning, development and operations of health care facilities and comprehensive delivery systems. Combines leadership success in:

- Integrated Health Care Delivery
- Staffing, Training & Development
- Budgeting & Cost Reduction
- Project & Time Management

- Government Relations & Liaison Affairs
- Contract Negotiations & Mediation
- Regulatory Reporting & Compliance
- Resource & Technology Acquisition

Excellent organizational, communications and analytical skills. Delivered innovative, cost-sensitive and high-quality managed care programs to replace traditional health care services. Adjunct University Professor.

PROFESSIONAL EXPERIENCE:

INMATE HEALTH SERVICES, INC.   1993 to Present
(National Contract Health Care Services Delivery Organization)

Regional Vice President - Wilmington, DE (1993 to Present)

Senior Executive with full responsibility for the strategic planning, staffing, financial affairs, resources, day-to-day operations and P&L performance of a comprehensive managed health care delivery system for the Wilmington Prison System. Operate six facilities delivering care to 5600 inmates and providing 100,000 clinic visits each year. Control $17 million annual operating budget. Direct a staff of 175 FTE's, Director of Nursing, Director of Medical Records, Regional Medical Director and administrative personnel. Provide oversight to a team of 20 physicians and 15 physician assistants.

- Delivered strong cost reductions in labor, material, equipment and overhead. Transitioned from breakeven in 1995 to 16% operating margin in 1996 with 10%+ projected for 1997.

- Spearheaded development of innovative health care services and programs including:
  - **In-House Specialty Health Care Practices** (e.g., general surgery, optometry, ophthalmology), reducing cost of services by an average of 5-7% annually.
  - **Managed Care** with a focus on cost reduction and quality control/assurance.
  - **Chronic Care** to reduce costs while improving quality of monitoring/management care.
  - **Pharmacy Utilization** to improve service and drug availability.

- Proactively managed litigation, medical malpractice and employee law. Worked closely with the City of Wilmington Law Department on consent decrees regarding medical care.

- Conceived/led in-house staff training and development programs on topics ranging from patient care standards to cost control, quality management and government liaison affairs.

- Structured and negotiated favorable union contracts and wage agreements.

- Established cooperative partnerships with the City of Wilmington Public Health Department and area hospitals to expand medical resources and provide timely follow-up of public health issues and referrals. Personally managed sensitive governmental and political liaison affairs.

INMATE HEALTH SERVICES, INC.*(Continued):*

Regional Manager - Atlanta, GA (1993)

Regional Health Care Administrator for the Sheriff's Department, three health care facilities and 3000 inmates. Directed a staff of five administrators/managers and 75 FTE's. Personally managed liaison affairs with local government agencies, attorneys, social service organizations and others.

- Led the organization through an aggressive restructuring, transitioning from loss to 18% profit within nine months. Resolved immediate crisis and restored client credibility.

- Resolved critical non-compliance issues with client contract, improved utilization management, implemented quality assurance initiatives and controlled overhead costs. Restaffed key management positions.

INSTITUTIONAL MEDICAL SERVICES, INC.   1990 to 1993
(National Contract Health Care Services Delivery Organization)

Health Service Administrator - Philadelphia, PA (1991 to 1993)

Orchestrated successful operating and financial turnaround of health care unit servicing the medical needs of 1200 inmates. Regained accreditation from the American Correctional Association following redesign and quality improvement of all service delivery and preventative care programs. Directed a staff of 35+.

Hospital Administrator - Greenville, SC (1990 to 1991)

Senior Administrator of a 35-bed inpatient care hospital within the confines of the South Carolina State Penitentiary. Full responsibility for facilities management, purchasing, budgeting, regulatory reporting, staffing and complete health care delivery system.

KAISER PERMANENTE HEALTH CARE PROGRAM, Rockville, MD   1979 to 1990

Medical Facility Administrator

Eleven-year management career with full P&L, operating, administrative, staffing and service delivery responsibility for a full-service outpatient health care facility, one of the earliest HMOs in the U.S. Serviced a population of more than 35,000 patients annually.

EDUCATION:

Executive Development Program, Stanford University, 1989

Masters of Public Administration, University of Virginia, 1979
Minor in Health Care Administration & Finance. Dean's List.

Bachelor of Business Administration, University of Virginia, 1976
Minor in Economics. Dean's List.

HOSPITALITY

Positions

Assistant Food & Beverage (F&B) Manager

Banquet Captain

Banquet Manager

Banquet Sales Manager

Certified Food & Beverage Executive (CFBE)

Certified Hotel Administrator (CHA)

Club Manager

Conference Center Manager

Director of Food & Beverage (F&B) Operations

District Manager

Food & Beverage (F&B) Manager

General Manager

Guest Services Manager

Marketing Manager

Multi-Unit Operations Manager

Operations Manager

Regional Director

Resort Manager

Restaurant Manager

Rooms Division Manager

Sales Director

Sales Manager

Unit Manager

KeyWords

Amenities - Created a world-class **amenities** program to attract VIPs, corporate executives and other business travelers.

Back-of-the-House Operations - Redesigned **back-of-the-house operations**, implemented incentives to support customer service objectives, and delivered a 12% reduction in annual operating costs.

Banquet Operations - Expanded service programs to include full-scale **banquet operations**, catered food service and other special events.

Budget Administration - Directed **budget administration**, forecasting and allocation for over $34 million in annual guest service expenses.

Catering Operations - Expanded on-premise **catering operations** to include major off-premise events for the Baltimore Orioles, Baltimore Convention Center and National Aquarium.

Club Management - Offer over 20 years experience in **club management** with exclusive private properties throughout Austria, Switzerland and Germany.

Conference Management - Recruited to plan, design, construct, staff and operate the first-ever **conference management** center in Nigeria ($8.8 million joint public-private venture).

Contract F&B Operations - Negotiated over $20 million in **contract F&B operations** for corporate centers in Atlanta, Charleston and Tampa.

Corporate Dining Room - Profitably operated the 200-seat **corporate dining room** at Federal Express headquarters.

Customer Service - Pioneered innovative **customer service** standards unique to the hospitality industry and successfully positioned Abrams Hotels as #1 in exclusive guest amenities.

Customer Retention - Designed promotional and marketing communications to improve **customer retention** in the group and business travel markets.

Food & Beverage Operations (F&B) - Senior Executive with full P&L responsibility for the entire **food & beverage operation** of Lyman Hotels worldwide (2000 properties in 84 countries on 5 continents).

Food Cost Controls - Implemented stringent **food cost controls** and reduced annual expenditures by $2+ million.

Front-of-the-House Operations - Created unique customer incentives and standards that drove strong gains in customer service throughout all **front-of-the-house operations**.

Guest Retention - Created and launched the "Guest Value" program that increased **guest retention** by more than 30% over two years.

Guest Satisfaction - Demonstrated the worth of "Guest Value" (unique customer service and loyalty program) with an average 95% **guest satisfaction** rating.

Hospitality Management - Built and operated profitable **hospitality management** programs worldwide for Hyatt, Hilton and several prestigious European properties.

Inventory Planning/Control - Forecasted annual product requirements and directed departmental **inventory planning and control** functions.

Labor Cost Controls - Restructured front- and back-of-the-house staffs, implemented stringent **labor cost controls** and saved $4.5+ million annually.

Meeting Planning - Directed **meeting planning** for annual sales conventions for major corporate clients (e.g., IBM, Xerox, 3M, Andersen, Gould).

Member Development/Retention - Launched unique print and broadcast advertising programs, direct mail campaigns and other communications to accelerate **member development** and improve **member retention**.

Menu Planning - Directed **menu planning** for more than 200 special event programs at Madison Square Garden (total cost of more than $75 million).

Menu Pricing - Restructured **menu pricing** and improved profit on average ticket by 5%.

Multi-Unit Operations - Held full responsibility for **multi-unit operations** through Wisconsin, Iowa and Minnesota (total of 250 employees and over $45 million in annual sales).

Occupancy - Improved **occupancy** ratings by 27% within the highly competitive corporate travel market in Chicago.

Portion Control - Standardized **portion control** procedures to reduce escalating costs.

Property Development - Management team representative for **property development** and construction programs of hotels, restaurants and conference centers throughout emerging Latin American markets.

Purchasing - Managed over $300 million in annual food and beverage **purchasing**.

Resort Management - Senior Operating Executive with full P&L responsibility for **resort management** and operations at six properties in the Western Caribbean.

Service Management - Spearheaded customer-driven **service management** and improvement programs to sustain competitive market lead.

Signature Property - Built and operated the 345-room Belvedere Property in Munich, Germany, creating what is now recognized as the Lederre Hotel Group's **signature property**.

Vendor Sourcing - Expanded **vendor sourcing**, identified low-cost suppliers and reduced overall purchasing costs by 8%-10% annually.

VIP Relations - Introduced top-flight **VIP relations** and amenities services catering to high net worth individuals and corporate executives on long-term travel assignments.

JOHN P. LANDAU, CHA
3859 Wabash Avenue #12B
Chicago, Illinois 60616
(847) 437-8621

HOSPITALITY INDUSTRY EXECUTIVE
Private Clubs, Hotels and F&B Operations

- Member Development & Retention
- Sales/Marketing Management
- Quality Customer Service
- Human Resource Affairs

- Finance/Budget Administration
- Project Management
- Marketing Pricing/Analysis
- New Product/Service Development

Consistently successful in increasing revenues, member service/satisfaction and profitability.

DISTINGUISHING CREDENTIALS:

- **Certified Hotel Administrator**, 1990
- Fluent English, French (mother tongue) and Spanish. Conversational German.
- Proficient in the use of PC-based lodging, reservation, F&B and financial management systems.

PROFESSIONAL EXPERIENCE:

CHICAGO ATHLETIC CLUB, Chicago, Illinois   1991 to Present

Manager

Senior Operations Executive with full management responsibility for the Club's member-only, 3-star hotel (218 rooms and suites). Direct all related staffing, guest service, pricing, financial analysis/reporting, quality and property management operations. Consult with Board and F&B management personnel to coordinate integrated operations, service and marketing programs.

- Initiated a series of operational improvements which increased revenue from $2.9 million in 1991 to $4.8 million (66% gain) in 1996. Improved bottom-line profitability by $1.9 million (135%).

- Designed and led several high-caliber service and management training programs.

- Launched the introduction of new quality and performance standards, in conjunction with supporting program of employee incentives and recognition.

Concurrently, serve as Manager of the Travelers Island Facility for the past two years. Hold full operating and P&L responsibility for the facility (18 tennis courts, pro shop, dining room, terrace, snack and cocktail lounge, bath house and 120-berth marina), guest/member relations and service quality. Drive forward efforts to enhance member service and retention.

- Authored new policies and procedures manual, realigned staffing patterns, implemented a series of cost reduction initiatives, and closed 1996 with expenses less than 1993.

- Created a service, quality and procedures training program for newly-hired personnel.

HOTEL LESTER, Chicago, Illinois   1990 to 1991
(Hotel Member of Relais & Chateaux)

Resident Manager

Full P&L responsibility for one of the most exclusive properties in Chicago (68 full-service suites). Directed the entire operation, all financial affairs, all facilities management programs and the complete F&B operation (including main dining room, room service and banquet facilities). Achieved a significant increase in banquet sales through personal negotiation and management of key customer relationships. Operated within the highest standards for quality and service.

SUNRISE HOTELS INTERNATIONAL   1985 to 1989

Hotel Manager / Project Manager, Chicago, Illinois (1988 to 1989)

Special Projects Director managing a diversity of corporate assignments involving new property development, property acquisition/feasibility analysis, and property turnaround/reorganization. Supervised financial analysis, prepared cash flow projections and debt service proformas, and provided financial support for potential acquisitions in Florida, New York and South Carolina.

- Directed a complete renovation and re-opening of the Sunrise Hotel in Boca Raton.

- Wrote corporate operations manual for affiliated hotels and restaurants.

Resident Manager, Sunrise Hotel, Chicago, Illinois (1985 to 1988)

Directed operations of this 3-star, 368-room, 220-employee hotel and of a large F&B operation (two restaurants, one bar and seven banquet rooms). Led a 5-person senior management team. Directed human resources, labor relations, training, purchasing, budgeting, guest relations, security, facilities and daily business operations. Managed strategic planning and execution of sales, marketing and business development campaigns.

- Contributed to dramatic growth and expansion with revenue increasing 135% to over $9.5 million and gross operating profit increasing 700% to $3.5 million.

- Directed $4.5 million renovation of the TowerSuite (12 units) and four banquet rooms.

HYATT INTERNATIONAL   1970 to 1985

Area Operations Analyst, Caribbean-Central America (1979 to 1985)

Unique management assignment conducting ongoing operational, profit, quality and performance reviews of the seven Hyatt properties in the Caribbean-Central American Region. Worked cooperatively with on-site management teams to facilitate operational improvements.

- Initiated changes in work procedures, departmental responsibilities and administrative systems that saved thousands of manhours per year and reduced net operating costs by $500,000+.

- Launched the introduction of several well-targeted quality and service enhancements.

Hotel Operations Analyst, Caracas Hyatt, Caracas, Venezuela (1975 to 1978)
Purchasing Director / F&B Controller, Bogota Hyatt, Bogota, Colombia (1970 to 1975)

EDUCATION: **Diploma - Ecole Hoteliere S.S.H.**, Lausanne, Switzerland
                       Diploma - Business Management, Lausanne, Switzerland
                       Financial Management Executive Training Program, Cornell University
                       Certified Hotel Administrator, American Hotel & Motel Association

HUMAN RESOURCES

Positions

Benefits & Compensation Administrator
Certified Professional in Human Resources (PHR)
Certified Senior Professional in Human Resources (SPHR)
Certified Trainer
Chief Human Resources Officer
Corporate Recruiter
Country Human Resources Manager
Director of Human Resources
Director of Organization(al) Development
Employee Assistance Program (EAP) Manager
EEO Specialist
Employee Relations Manager
Employment Manager
Employment Specialist
Human Resources Generalist
Human Resources Manager
Human Resources Representative
Human Resources Specialist
International Employment Manager
International Human Resources Director
Labor Relations Specialist
Management Development Specialist
Management Recruiter
Manager of Management Resources
Manpower Planning Manager
Organization(al) Development Director
Pension Plan Administrator

Personnel Administrator
Personnel Division Director
Personnel Manager
Professional Recruiter
Recruiter
Staffing Manager
Technical Employment Manager
Training & Development Manager
Vice President of Human Resources
Vice President of Organization(al) Development
Wage & Salary Analyst
Training Specialist

KeyWords

American Disabilities Act (ADA) - Expanded regulatory compliance programs to incorporate new federal **ADA** regulations and initiated $12 million capital investment program to upgrade facilities to meet access requirements.

Benefits Administration - Expanded in-house **benefits administration** function to include pension plans, 401(k) plans, tuition reimbursement programs, LOA programs and joint spouse maternity leave programs.

Career Pathing - Introduced the concepts of **career pathing**, leadership development and succession planning into Federal Express in an effort to increase executive staff recruitment and retention.

Change Management - Pioneered innovative **change management** programs focused on core productivity, efficiency and safety improvement programs.

Claims Administration - Directed a 12-person **claims administration** function responsible for all health insurance, disability and workers' compensation claims.

College Recruitment - Managed a nationwide **college recruitment** program to attract talented young engineers and technical designers.

Compensation - Benchmarked best practices worldwide to create Knudsen's domestic and international **compensation** programs.

Competency-Based Performance - Created a **competency-based performance** analysis and appraisal system to identify top performers and facilitate progressive career movement.

Corporate Culture Change - Pioneered **corporate culture change** initiatives impacting more than 10,000 employees at 54 manufacturing facilities and 122 sales offices throughout Europe, Asia and Latin America.

Cross-Cultural Communications - Introduced in-house language training programs to strengthen staff competencies in **cross-cultural communications**.

Diversity Management - Forged the introduction of **diversity management** programs and initiatives to expand hiring, training and promotion of minority candidates.

Equal Employment Opportunity (EEO) - Achieved/surpassed all **EEO** and Affirmative Action regulations.

Employee Communications - Designed and produced multimedia **employee communications** for new hire orientation, training and leadership development.

Employee Empowerment - Championed implementation of **employee empowerment** and participative management programs to increase management/staff relations and cooperation.

Employee Involvement Teams - Formed six **employee involvement teams** to support HR's efforts in employee downsizing, reorganization and consolidation.

Employee Relations - Expanded **employee relations** initiatives to include in-house EAP and counseling programs.

Employee Retention - Designed performance-based incentives for a 200-person hourly workforce and increased **employee retention** by better than 26%.

Employee Surveys - Wrote, administered and reported results of corporate-wide **employee surveys** investigating employee satisfaction and personal career objectives.

Expatriate Employment - Spearheaded a worldwide **expatriate employment** and human resources function incorporating recruitment, training and development, succession planning and compensation.

Grievance Proceedings - Administered over 100 **grievance proceedings** as the direct intermediary between union and management officials.

Human Resources (HR) - Senior Executive with full operating responsibility for design, development and leadership of comprehensive **human resources** and organization development function.

Human Resources Generalist Affairs - Administered all **HR generalist affairs** including recruitment, selection, training, manpower planning, benefits, claims administration, employee relations and succession planning.

Human Resources Partnerships - Forged innovative **human resources partnerships** with key operating divisions worldwide to drive common vision and achieve financial objectives.

Incentive Planning - Spearheaded **incentive planning** functions for sales and support personnel through ITI's worldwide field organization.

International Employment - Created a comprehensive **international employment** organization responsible for all generalist HR functions and a complex expatriate compensation program.

Job Task Analysis - Conducted a sophisticated **job task analysis** study to delineate all core competencies, functions and requirements of each of the company's 22 different job classifications.

Labor Arbitration - Negotiated favorable resolutions to several high-profile **labor arbitration** proceedings negatively impacting Bethlehem Steel's long-term market viability.

Labor Contract Negotiations - Directed 6-person cross-functional team responsible for **labor contract negotiations** with Teamsters officials.

Labor Relations - Created a proactive **labor relations** function that successfully thwarted several work stoppages and proposed walk-outs.

Leadership Assessment - Developed quantifiable tools for **leadership assessment** of top operating management.

Leadership Development - Pioneered innovative **leadership development** programs to accelerate career advancement of high-potential management candidates.

Management Training & Development - Identified organizational needs and created a 4-part **management training and development program**.

Manpower Planning - Created **manpower planning** methodologies to staff new production facilities in Iowa and Utah.

Merit Promotion - Designed a performance-driven **merit promotion** program to reward top producers.

Multimedia Training - Partnered with Technology Services Division to create **multimedia training** and leadership programs integrating voice, data and other electronic systems.

Multinational Workforce - Managed a 42-person **multinational workforce** with personnel from Germany, Switzerland, Austria, Japan, Mexico and the U.S.

Organization(al) Design - Defined new corporate vision and established new **organizational design** to streamline management tiers and advance staff to supervisory positions.

Organization(al) Development (OD) - Spearheaded **OD** initiatives incorporating change management, employee empowerment, participative leadership and process reengineering.

Organization(al) Needs Assessment - Conducted worldwide **organizational needs assessment** to define core drivers in fast-paced technology industries.

Participative Management - Energized staff and supervisors to successfully transition to **participative management** organizational structure.

Performance Appraisal - Created a comprehensive **performance appraisal** system based on pre-established performance criteria.

Performance Incentives - Designed a complete portfolio of **performance incentives** awarded for measurable gains in production yield, quality performance and customer satisfaction.

Performance Reengineering - Led fast-paced **performance reengineering** initiatives to keep pace with rapid market expansion and customer growth.

Position Classification - Designed a corporate-wide **position classification** system with associated salary grades, levels and incentive structures.

Professional Recruitment - Spearheaded an aggressive **professional recruitment** program to identify top industry performers in sales, marketing and international business development.

Regulatory Affairs - Administered **regulatory affairs**, compliance and reporting with state and federal agencies governing HR operations.

Retention - Designed staff incentives and increased employee **retention** by better than 45%.

Safety Training - Accelerated the corporation's commitment to safe work practices with the introduction of a plant-wide **safety training** program.

Self-Directed Work Teams - Created **self-directed work teams** responsible for full product line management, from initial R&D through manufacturing and customer delivery.

Staffing - Redefined **staffing** levels to assimilate new technologies and reduce annual payroll expenditures.

Succession Planning - Created **succession planning** models adopted by national association as best in practices model for the entire industry.

Train-the-Trainer - Developed curriculum and instructional materials for **train-the-trainer** programs in technology, telecommunications and electronic commerce.

Training & Development - Planned and launched start-up of worldwide **training and development** division to support the company's expansion into emerging product technologies and markets.

Union Negotiations - Led sensitive **union negotiations** governing salary and benefit programs for all two million members of the United Autoworkers Union.

Union Relations - Forged positive **union relations** through cooperative design of safe work practices and full compensation for on-the-job injuries.

Wage & Salary Administration - Developed a corporate-wide **wage and salary administration** program to ensure equitable compensation across all geographies and job classifications.

Workforce Reengineering - Led a massive **workforce reengineering** initiative to reduce Terminal's worldwide staff by 30% by the end of 1999.

BENJAMIN F. SMITH
9348 Pioneer Square #4
Seattle, Washington 98332
Home (206) 356-8732   Office (206) 983-3252

PROFESSIONAL QUALIFICATIONS:

PROJECT MANAGER / COUNSELOR / ADMINISTRATOR / HUMAN SERVICES PROFESSIONAL
experienced in the design, planning and delivery of programs for substance abusers, criminal offenders, economically disadvantaged, handicapped and other special needs populations. Qualifications include:

- Strong skills in proposal writing, public speaking and program management
- Well-developed counseling, communications and crisis management skills.
- Over 10 years of general business and administrative management experience.
- Extensive qualifications in personnel training and supervision, budgeting, resource/funds allocation and docu-
  mentation/recordkeeping.

PROFESSIONAL EXPERIENCE:

Volunteer Additions Counselor   1993 to Present
THE HAVEN, Seattle, Washington

Provide individual counseling to substance abusers at this drug and alcohol outpatient facility. Work with
clients referred by the courts, social workers, rehabilitation centers and other human service agencies/
professionals. Design individualized treatment plans and objectives, maintain/update all client documentation, consult with Director regarding case management, coordinate crisis intervention services and expedite
external referrals for inpatient admissions.

- Assist Director with the preparation of fund raising solicitations to support program operations and
  service expansion.
- Designed and implemented effective counseling programs designed specifically to meet the needs of a
  diverse client population with various substance addictions.

Co-Owner & Field Service Manager   1986 to Present
HEATING SUPPLY, Seattle, Washington

Own and operate a heating contracting business that has become a leader in furnace retrofit and installation
work in the Seattle metro area. Prepare work orders and estimates, schedule and supervise work crews,
coordinate equipment and material acquisitions, and manage customer service/relations.

- Increased company sales 500% since 1987.
- Wrote proposals, capabilities statements and operating plans to secure government contracts.

Project Manager   1981 to 1986
INSTITUTE FOR HUMAN DEVELOPMENT, Seattle, Washington

Directed a large-scale furnace retrofit pilot project undertaken as part of the Institute's program to assist Seattle's economically disadvantaged citizens. Demonstrated average fuel savings of 21% on initial 200 installations and authored final report which was instrumental in changing federal legislation concerning the use of energy assistance funds.

- Prepared documentation, negotiated and secured funding from private foundations and local government to continue agency operations.
- Managed $2 million annual energy conservation project that completed 8000+ heating system retrofits in four years. Supervised a staff of 12 field and administrative personnel in addition to 30+ contractors.

Volunteer Proposal Writer   1983
LYNWOOD PRISON, Lynwood, Washington

Authored winning proposal to establish a skills training program (e.g., carpentry, plumbing, home repair, building maintenance) on-site at Lynwood Prison. Determined budget, staffing, material and other resource requirements to develop in-house training curriculum and fully-equipped shop. Wrote training curriculum, program objectives, schedules and skills performance criteria.

- Prepared proposal that was successfully funded by local government and operated by the prison for several years.

Senior Planner   1974 to 1980
OFFICE OF EMPLOYMENT & TRAINING, Seattle, Washington

Wrote annual plan to provide the unemployed and economically disadvantaged citizens of Seattle with skills, vocational and educational training opportunities. Surveyed local economic trends, industry trends and labor shortages to determine appropriate training programs offered by public and private organizations throughout the region. Consulted with Director regarding funding approval and policy recommendations. Supervised research, strategic planning and program development activities.

- Wrote several proposals that won in national competition and brought an additional $20 million in discretionary funding to the City. Proposals included special training programs for the handicapped, offenders, welfare recipients and non-native English language speakers.
- Designed a public awareness program to educate the local business community and improve employment opportunities for ex-offenders. Hosted several high-profile business meetings and seminars, coordinated media coverage and launched a series of public education initiatives.

EDUCATION:

M.A., Economics, University of Washington, 1974
B.A., Economics, Seattle Pacific University, 1971
Postgraduate Courses, Psychology & Psychotherapy, University of Washington, 1992 and 1993

HUMAN SERVICES

Positions

Administrator
Agency Director
Agency Manager
Associate Director
Behavioral Specialist
Case Worker
Client Advocate
Clinician
Counselor
Director of Human Services
Director of Social Services
Executive Director
Human Services Professional
Human Services Specialist
Psychiatrist
Psychologist
Rehabilitation Specialist
Service Delivery Manager
Social Services Administrator
Social Worker
Substance Abuse Counselor
Vocational Evaluator

KeyWords

Adult Services - Expanded traditional programming to include a complete portfolio of **adult services** (e.g., in-home healthcare, sports, recreation, daycare).

Advocacy - Spearheaded regional **advocacy** to increase awareness of the need for expanded human services, counseling and substance abuse programs.

Behavior Management - Created an integrated **behavior management** model demonstrated to offset the impact of Turret's Disease on unintended vocalizations.

Behavior Modification - Innovated **behavior modification** programs successful in controlling the physical outbursts of dually-diagnosed adolescent clients.

Casework - Directed all **casework** planning, staff assignment and client review proceedings prior to court appearances.

Client Advocacy - Forged aggressive **client advocacy** programs to expand vocational training opportunities through state-funded agencies.

Client Placement - Administered **client placement** in mental health and rehabilitation facilities throughout the State of New Jersey.

Community-Based Intervention - Organized **community-based intervention** for repeat offenders indigenous to the local area.

Community Outreach - Spearheaded successful **community outreach** programs linking local residents with privately-funded and publicly-administered human service programs.

Counseling - Directed clinical intervention teams responsible for individual, group and family **counseling** in state-wide residential facilities.

Crisis Intervention - Directed **crisis intervention** with potentially suicidal patients in a state-funded facility.

Diagnostic Evaluation - Managed interdisciplinary medical and nursing team responsible for comprehensive **diagnostic evaluation** of all incoming clients.

Discharge Planning - Coordinated cross-functional medical, nursing, rehabilitative and counseling team managing **discharge planning** and follow-up care.

Dually Diagnosed - Conducted a longitudinal research study of **dually diagnosed** children through adolescence and adulthood to identify common characteristics and effective treatment protocols.

Group Counseling - Facilitated **group counseling** sessions with inmates from correctional institutions throughout the state system.

Human Services - Senior Executive with full responsibility for the strategic planning, staffing, budgeting and administration of a large **human services** organization.

Independent Life Skills Training - Developed novel strategies to improve programs for **independent life skills training** and living.

Inpatient - Increased reimbursable income from **inpatient** population by 23% over two years.

Integrated Service Delivery - Assembled cross-functional clinical team to provide a centralized program for **integrated service delivery**.

Mainstreaming - Advocated and won legislative support for introduction of educational **mainstreaming** programs.

Outpatient - Controlled $250 million in private donations allocated for the delivery of comprehensive **outpatient services** to elderly residents of the inner city.

Program Development - Spearheaded strategic alliances with research centers and universities nationwide to facilitate **program development**, delivery and success.

Protective Services - Issued judicial orders for **protective services** in alleged cases of child and sexual abuse.

Psychoanalysis - Completed 12 years of in-depth **psychoanalysis** with leading psychiatrists utilizing both traditional and non-traditional therapies.

Psychological Counseling - Managed healthcare team responsible for **psychological counseling**, crisis intervention and long-term treatment planning.

Psychotropic Medication - Authorized to dispense **psychotropic medication** in emergency situations.

School Counseling - Founded and managed Wisconsin State's **School Counseling** and Health Services program.

Social Services - Directed a 200-employee **social services** organization with $100 million in annual funding from government, not-for-profit and private organizations.

Social Welfare - Lobbied for the successful passage of favorable **social welfare** designed to obliterate the region's rapidly expanding inner city problems.

Substance Abuse - Designed proactive **substance abuse** and rehabilitation programs that were successful in reducing the negative behaviors associated with prolonged addiction.

Testing - Administered a comprehensive psychological, emotional, cognitive and behavioral **testing** program.

Treatment Planning - Coordinated **treatment planning** and intervention for both inpatient and outpatient populations.

Vocational Rehabilitation - Designed the first-ever **vocational rehabilitation** programs in cooperation with Xerox, IBM, Westinghouse, AlliedSignal and other major corporations.

Vocational Placement - Coordinated **vocational placement** for all incoming program participants.

Vocational Testing - Designed **vocational testing** tools to accurately identify each individual's technical, analytical and mechanical competencies.

Youth Training Program - Forged strategic partnerships with area colleges and universities for an innovative **youth training program** designed to advance the educational standards and expectations of the local population.

BENJAMIN F. SMITH
9348 Pioneer Square #4
Seattle, Washington 98332
Home (206) 356-8732   Office (206) 983-3252

PROFESSIONAL QUALIFICATIONS:

PROJECT MANAGER / COUNSELOR / ADMINISTRATOR / HUMAN SERVICES

PROFESSIONAL experienced in the design, planning and delivery of programs for substance abusers, criminal offenders, economically disadvantaged, handicapped and other special needs populations. Qualifications include:

- Strong skills in proposal writing, public speaking and program management
- Well-developed counseling, communications and crisis management skills.
- Over 10 years of general business and administrative management experience.
- Extensive qualifications in personnel training and supervision, budgeting, resource/funds allocation and documentation/recordkeeping.

PROFESSIONAL EXPERIENCE:

Volunteer Additions Counselor   1993 to Present
THE HAVEN, Seattle, Washington

Provide individual counseling to substance abusers at this drug and alcohol outpatient facility. Work with clients referred by the courts, social workers, rehabilitation centers and other human service agencies/professionals. Design individualized treatment plans and objectives, maintain/update all client documentation, consult with Director regarding case management, coordinate crisis intervention services and expedite external referrals for inpatient admissions.

- Assist Director with the preparation of fund raising solicitations to support program operations and service expansion.
- Designed and implemented effective counseling programs designed specifically to meet the needs of a diverse client population with various substance addictions.

Co-Owner & Field Service Manager   1986 to Present
HEATING SUPPLY, Seattle, Washington

Own and operate a heating contracting business that has become a leader in furnace retrofit and installation work in the Seattle metro area. Prepare work orders and estimates, schedule and supervise work crews, coordinate equipment and material acquisitions, and manage customer service/relations.

- Increased company sales 500% since 1987.
- Wrote proposals, capability statements and operating plans to secure government contracts.

Project Manager   1981 to 1986
INSTITUTE FOR HUMAN DEVELOPMENT, Seattle, Washington

Directed a large-scale furnace retrofit pilot project undertaken as part of the Institute's program to assist Seattle's economically disadvantaged citizens. Demonstrated average fuel savings of 21% on initial 200 installations and authored final report which was instrumental in changing federal legislation concerning the use of energy assistance funds.

- Prepared documentation, negotiated and secured funding from private foundations and local government to continue agency operations.
- Managed $2 million annual energy conservation project that completed 8000+ heating system retrofits in four years. Supervised a staff of 12 field and administrative personnel in addition to 30+ contractors.

Volunteer Proposal Writer   1983
LYNWOOD PRISON, Lynwood, Washington

Authored winning proposal to establish a skills training program (e.g., carpentry, plumbing, home repair, building maintenance) on-site at Lynwood Prison. Determined budget, staffing, material and other resource requirements to develop in-house training curriculum and fully-equipped shop. Wrote training curriculum, program objectives, schedules and skills performance criteria.

- Prepared proposal that was successfully funded by local government and operated by the prison for several years.

Senior Planner   1974 to 1980
OFFICE OF EMPLOYMENT & TRAINING, Seattle, Washington

Wrote annual plan to provide the unemployed and economically disadvantaged citizens of Seattle with skills, vocational and educational training opportunities. Surveyed local economic trends, industry trends and labor shortages to determine appropriate training programs offered by public and private organizations throughout the region. Consulted with Director regarding funding approval and policy recommendations. Supervised research, strategic planning and program development activities.

- Wrote several proposals that won in national competition and brought an additional $20 million in discretionary funding to the City. Proposals included special training programs for the handicapped, offenders, welfare recipients and non-native English language speakers.
- Designed a public awareness program to educate the local business community and improve employment opportunities for ex-offenders. Hosted several high-profile business meetings and seminars, coordinated media coverage and launched public education initiatives.

EDUCATION:

M.A., Economics, University of Washington, 1974
B.A., Economics, Seattle Pacific University, 1971
Postgraduate Courses, Psychology & Psychotherapy, University of Washington, 1992 and 1993

INFORMATION SYSTEMS & TELECOMMUNICATIONS TECHNOLOGY

Positions

Applications Development Analyst

Applications Development Manager

Certified Computer Professional (CCP)

Chief Information Officer (CIO)

Communications Director

Computer Applications Engineer

Computer Analyst

Corporate Technology Director

Corporate Technology Officer

Data Administration Manager

Data Center Manager

Database Administrator

Database Manager

Director of Computer Operations

Director of End User Computing

Director of Information Management (IM)

Director of Software Development

Director of Technical Support Operations

Executive Vice President for Technology

Global Information Systems (IS) Manager

Global Information Technology (IT) Manager

Global Systems Director

Information Center Manager
Information Systems Administrator
Information Technology Director
Internet Technology Manager
Management Information Services (MIS) Director
Network Administrator
Network Development Analyst
Programming Manager
Project Leader
Project Manager
Research & Development (R&D) Director
Senior Information Systems Officer
Senior Project Manager
Senior Systems Analyst
Systems Administrator
Systems Analyst
Systems Engineer
Systems Manager
Systems Requirements Manager
Technology Systems Manager
Telecommunications Manager
Telecommunications Technology Director
Vice President of MIS
Vice President of Information Systems
Vice President of Information Technology
Vice President of Research & Technology
Vice President of Technology
Vice President of Voice & Data Communications

KeyWords

Advanced Technology - Recruited to Tandem Computers to spearhead the design, development and delivery of **advanced technology** solutions for major banks and financial institutions nationwide.

Applications Development - Led a 22-person **applications development** team designing new software programs to meet transactional requirements.

Architecture - Directed systems **architecture** design across multiple platforms to ensure optimum integration and information access.

Artificial Intelligence (AI) - Forged TI's launch into the emerging **AI** industry.

Automated Voice Response (AVR) - Introduced **AVR** technology to expedite customer support and field service operations.

Backbone - Designed ethernet **backbone** to support both LAN and WAN transmissions.

Benchmarking - Guided systems **benchmarking** across multiple industries, technologies and applications.

CASE Tools - Pioneered the introduction of **CASE tools** to further accelerate development of advanced systems technology.

Capacity Planning - Evaluated existing technologies and defined **capacity planning** requirements for the next five years.

CD-ROM Technology - Expanded Time-Life's product offerings to include **CD-ROM technology** for delivery of both print and video publications.

Cellular Communications - Built and managed a large-scale **cellular communications** sales and marketing division in partnership with AT&T.

Client/Server Architecture - Transitioned from mainframe to **client/server architecture** reducing systems costs by 15% and increasing systems accessibility by better than 25%.

Computer Science - Graduated top of the class from MIT with a joint **Computer Science** and Engineering degree.

Cross-Functional Technology Team - Led a 45-person **cross-functional technology team** challenged to build the company's first-ever telecommunications systems.

Data Communications - Managed a 24x7 **data communications** and data support center.

Data Center Operations - Supported **data center operations** worldwide with the introduction of emerging hardware, software and networking technologies.

Data Dictionary - Designed a comprehensive **data dictionary** for use by all technical and non-technical staff in their joint systems development efforts.

Data Recovery - Introduced time-sensitive **data recovery** processes and virtually eliminated all data losses.

Database Administration - Created a formal **data administration** function to control all IT development projects and daily systems operations.

Database Design - Led 6-person IT team in **database design** and documentation projects.

Database Server - Replaced obsolete technology with leading edge **database server**, expedited data processing and eliminated systems duplication.

Desktop Technology - Launched Xerox's entry into the rapidly expanding **desktop technology** market.

Disaster Recovery - Authored Seagrams' in-house **disaster recovery** processes.

Document Imaging - Forged strategic alliance with emerging technology venture to provide Octel with the latest advances in **document imaging** technology.

Electronic Data Interchange (EDI) - Spearheaded introduction of **EDI** technology with major retailers nationwide (e.g., Walmart, Sears, Target, Sam's Club).

Emerging Technologies - Senior Operating Executive challenged to revitalize operations and lead the corporation's launch into **emerging technologies** designed specifically for the healthcare and human services industries.

Electronic Mail (Email) - Introduced **email** to improve headquarters communications with field sales teams worldwide.

End User Support - Expanded help desk staff to strengthen **end user support** programs.

Enterprise Systems - Advised senior executives regarding the functionality and utility of **enterprise systems** technology.

Expert Systems - Led design and development of **expert systems** for sophisticated data collection, analysis and reporting processes.

Fault Analysis - Created the industry's first **fault analysis** technology, now a $2 billion revenue center for Xytoc Computer Systems.

Field Support - Restaffed and retrained **field support** team to improve quality of customer technology installations and technical training.

Fourth Generation Language - Developed **fourth generation language** used in advanced scientific applications.

Frame Relay - Transitioned to **frame relay** technology to accelerate MIS capabilities.

Geographic Information System (GIS) - Pioneered the use of **GIS** technology in the UPS global organization.

Global Systems Support - Established new business unit to provide **global systems support** to AI users worldwide.

Graphical User Interface (GUI) - Developed **GUI** application to merge common technologies across diverse platforms.

Hardware Configuration - Directed engineering team responsible for **hardware configuration** and field installation at customer sites.

Hardware Development/Engineering - Redesigned **hardware development and engineering** protocols in response to changing user requirements.

Help Desk - Staffed and operated a 24x7 **help desk** supporting both internal and external customers.

Host-Based System - Reengineered **host-based system** to accommodate new technology installations and upgrades.

Imaging Technology - Negotiated $12 million acquisition of advanced **imaging technology**.

Information Technology (IT) - Senior **IT** Executive with full operating and systems planning responsibility for a newly-formed technology consortium between Tandem and Carnegie Mellon.

Internet - Forged PacBell's profitable entry into the emerging **Internet** market.

Joint Application Development (JAD) - Accelerated **JAD** projects with the introduction of an experienced front-line technology management team.

Local Area Network (LAN) - Invested over $3 million to develop **LAN** technology to link all corporate sales offices and distribution centers.

Management Information Systems (MIS) - Senior **MIS** Executive with full P&L responsibility for Allied's $400 million Technology Systems Division.

Multimedia Technology - Introduced **multimedia technology** (e.g., electronic commerce, videoconferencing, CD-ROM, Internet) to capitalize upon high-growth market opportunities.

Multiuser Interface - Designed **multiuser interface** to expand systems capabilities.

Multivendor Systems Integration - Orchestrated a complex **multivendor systems integration** project to deliver advanced navigational technologies to the U.S. Armed Forces.

Network Administration - Senior Manager responsible for **network administration**, technology acquisitions, budgeting, staffing and performance improvement.

Object Oriented - Advanced **object oriented** systems technologies into non-traditional development projects.

Office Automation (OA) - Forged strategic alliance with DRG Computers to deliver **OA** technology throughout the Department of Energy, Department of Commerce and U.S. State Department.

Online - Accelerated development of **online** technology to keep pace with regional and national competition.

Operating System - Redefined **operating system** requirements to upgrade technology performance and strengthen data quality.

Parallel Systems Operations - Managed **parallel systems operations** during conversion from IBM to Digital equipment.

PC Technology - Replaced obsolete mainframes with advanced **PC technology**.

Pilot Implementation - Managed **pilot implementation** of new AI and robotics technologies.

Process Modeling - Orchestrated a large-scale **process modeling** project in preparation for new technology installation.

Project Lifecycle - Administered **project lifecycle** from initial systems planning and technology acquisition through installation, training and operations.

Project Management Methodology - Defined **project management methodology** to optimize technology resources and applications.

Rapid Application Development (RAD) - Facilitated introduction of **RAD** processes to expedite systems implementation.

Real Time Data - Created platform for **real time data** collection, analysis and worldwide dissemination.

Relational Database - Designed **relational database** technology as part of the corporation's transition to advanced systems operation.

Remote Systems Access - Developed technology to provide **remote systems access** for sites worldwide.

Research & Development (R&D) - Planned, staffed, budgeted and directed operations of a sophisticated technology **R&D** center.

Resource Management - Controlled **resource management** and allocation of $100 million in hardware, software and network technologies.

Software Configuration - Pioneered innovative **software configuration** models that led to a major evolution within the financial software industry.

Software Development/Engineering - Led 22-person cross-functional project team challenged to revitalize and expand **software development and engineering** capabilities.

Systems Acquisition - Negotiated over $50 million in **systems acquisitions** to fund expansion and diversification.

Systems Configuration - Managed **systems configuration** for all new technology acquisitions and internal development projects.

Systems Development Methodology - Reengineered **systems development methodology** to integrated CASE tools, AI and fourth generation language.

Systems Documentation - Led team responsible for technical and non-technical **systems documentation**.

Systems Engineering - Directed a team of Ph.D. scientists in the development of **systems engineering** processes, protocols and standards.

Systems Functionality - Tested operations to ensure optimum **systems functionality** and availability.

Systems Implementation - Guided **systems implementation** across multiple platforms at 34 locations.

Systems Integration - Elevated the stature of the **systems integration** team with the provision of service-driven, quality-driven customer performance standards.

Systems Security - Introduced leading edge **systems security** and intellectual property protection technologies.

Technical Documentation - Revised all **technical documentation** governing client/server architectures and systems operations.

Technical Training - Wrote curriculum, trained instructors and directed **technical training** programs for user groups nationwide.

Technology Commercialization - Transitioned EL Labs from an R&D facility into an advanced **technology commercialization** organization.

Technology Integration - Spearheaded **technology integration** of all new system acquisitions and in-house development projects.

Technology Licensing - Negotiated over $200 million in **technology licensing** and transfer agreements with business partners throughout Asia Pacific.

Technology Needs Assessment - Conducted organization-wide **technology needs assessment** for Andersen's Global Consulting Division.

Technology Rightsizing - Revitalized operations and led an aggressive **technology rightsizing** effort to divest non-essential assets.

Technology Solutions - Pioneered **technology solutions** to meet the needs of complex customer service, logistics and distribution operations.

Technology Transfer - Established strategic alliances with major R&D facilities nationwide and coordinated **technology transfer** between researchers and commercial systems vendors.

Telecommunications Technology - Credited with the development, engineering and market launch of advanced **telecommunications technology** integrating LAN, WAN and satellite systems.

Teleconferencing Technology - Saved the corporation $4 million in travel expenses through implementation of in-house **teleconferencing technology**.

User Training & Support - Recognized for success in the delivery of **user training and support** programs that outpaced the competition and provided 24-hour support to customers nationwide.

Vendor Partnerships - Structured and negotiated **vendor partnerships** to facilitate joint systems development projects.

Voice Communications - Acquired AT&T's premier systems to enhance **voice communications** technologies.

Wide Area Network (WAN) - Invested over $2.8 million in **WAN** technology to link operating divisions worldwide.

MARILYN P. CLAYTON
1520 Main Street
Colorado Springs, Colorado 82160

Phone: (303) 402-3322   URL: http://www.technology/consult   Email: consult@aol.com

---

MULTIMEDIA TECHNOLOGIST & PROGRAM/PROJECT DIRECTOR
Delivering Advanced, PC- & UNIX-Based Programs, Systems & Technologies

Combines cross-functional, cross-technology experience in the design, staffing, budgeting and delivery of advanced systems and applications. Successful in developing and integrating technologies to support broad-ranging operating, financial and organizational needs. Core competencies include:

- Multimedia Content Design
- Computer-Based Training & Authoring
- Program Development & Management
- Product Development & Marketing

- Interactive Technology
- Technical & Non-Technical Training
- Cross-Functional Team Leadership
- Client Training & Management

TECHNOLOGY SKILLS & EXPERTISE:

Multimedia Authoring Tools
GAIN/Momentum (UNIX under Motif)
ICON Author (PC)
WISE (PC)
TICCIT (Digital)
TenCORE

WEB Site Development (Mac)
Netscape Navigator Gold
HTML

Office Productivity Tools (PC/Mac)
Microsoft Office (Word, Excel, PowerPoint)
Framemaker
Lotus Notes
ACT!
Filemaker Pro

Graphics Development Tools (Mac)
Adobe Acrobat/Illustrator
DeBabilizer

PROFESSIONAL EXPERIENCE:

MULTIMEDIA TECHNOLOGY CONSULTANT   1996 to Present

Independent Consultant specializing in the design, development and delivery of advanced, PC- and UNIX-based technology programs. Project highlights include:

- **Swedish Mobile** — Supported implementation of computer-based, interactive, training systems for American Management Systems' ForCe 2000 telecommunications software.
- **Sprint** — Managed needs analysis, design, navigation design, interface design (using lobbying/ building metaphor), Design Specification Document and prototype development for billing system training and technology support systems.

LRX INCORPORATED, Denver, Colorado   1992 to 1996

Product Director
Senior Director leading the development of an interactive, multimedia, computer-based training CD-ROM for a computer-aided design 3D modeling software program.

- Directed project from initial concept, feasibility and market analysis through development, pricing, staffing, training and software vendor partnership. Led cross-functional project team of designers, artists, programmers, editors and support staff.
- Defined systems approach, interface design, content and marketing strategies.
- Established 800 number technical support team, all marketing communications and promotions, user manuals and ACT! customer tracking database to support product launch.

MARILYN P. CLAYTON   Page Two

Senior Technology Designer
Subcontracted to Techniflight Corporation to develop a multimedia tutorial for Lear jet introductory flight training (using GAIN/Momentum UNIX-based authoring tool from Sybase). Subsequently contracted for full-time commitment to the FOCUS: Hope Project in Detroit, Michigan, an innovative, technologically-sophisticated University curriculum for the Center for Advanced Technology.

- Facilitated development of state-of-the-art engineering systems/strategies for CAD/CAM, tool crib controls and quality assurance applications.

RADIUM SYSTEMS, INC., Fairfax, Virginia   1985 to 1991

Group Manager & Senior Technology Designer
Joined Radium Systems as the first Instructional Designer in the corporation. Over the next six years, spearheaded the growth and expansion of the department to 21 professionals delivering UNIX-based, multimedia programs and technologies to government and commercial clients worldwide. Member of Corporate Strategic Planning Team.

- Introduced applied Instructional System Development (ISD) approach to design seven multimedia courses in advanced electronic systems deployment (total contract value exceeding $2.6 million). Computer-based training was integrated into an HP-based part task trainer.
- Performed human factors critical task analyses, wrote functional system requirements, and designed text and graphics.
- Led team in development/delivery of technology programs using PC-based WICAT authoring tool (WISE) to design integrated systems for the Republic of China Navy.
- Proposal Manager for 10+ competitive RFPs and Statement of Qualification documents.

Program Manager
Led development of three advanced technology programs valued from $500,000 to $7 million. Directed preparation of Statement of Work, managed customer negotiations, calculated labor and material costs, negotiated subcontractor and consulting agreements, and managed projects through to on-budget completion.

LOGISTIX, INC., Washington, D.C.   1983 to 1985

Staff Analyst
Developed technology training programs for workstations, word processing, spreadsheet, database, graphics and integration packages. Explored expert systems technology for job aid applications.

NATIONAL INFORMATION SYSTEMS, Baltimore, Maryland   1979 to 1984

Marketing Support Trainer
Programming Team Leader

EDUCATION:

Graduate Studies in Multimedia Development & Human Computer Interface Design
UNIVERSITY OF COLORADO

Graduate Studies in Human Factors Engineering & Industrial Psychology
THE AMERICAN UNIVERSITY

BS - English & Instructional Technology
THE AMERICAN UNIVERSITY

INTERNATIONAL BUSINESS DEVELOPMENT

Positions

Area Sales Executive

Business Development Director

Business Development Executive

Business Development Manager

Country Sales & Marketing Manager

Director of International Business Development

Director of International Trade

General Manager

Global Account Manager

Global Marketing Director

Global Sales Director

Global Trade Manager

Import / Export Manager

International Business Advisor

International Business Consultant

International Marketing Executive

International Sales Executive

Managing Director

Regional Sales & Marketing Director

Senior Vice President of Business Development

Senior Vice President of International Trade

Vice President of Global Sales & Marketing

Vice President of Import & Export Trade

KeyWords

Acquisition - Identified candidate, directed due diligence, structured transaction and negotiated the largest **acquisition** ($26.4 million) in the history of the corporation.

Barter Transactions - Pioneered Xytac's first-ever **barter transaction** programs to expand international trade opportunities.

Channel Development - Guided marketing and distributor **channel development** throughout emerging Latin American markets.

Competitive Intelligence - Created statistical models and reports of **competitive intelligence** for products, technologies, services and market reach.

Corporate Development - Championed **corporate development** initiatives including mergers, acquisitions, strategic alliances, joint ventures and co-marketing partnerships.

Cross-Border Transactions - Negotiated complex **cross-border transactions** between Vietnamese suppliers and Taiwanese distributors.

Cross-Cultural Communications - Developed training seminars to enhance the **cross-cultural communications** competencies of Xerox's international sales, marketing and service organizations.

Diplomatic Protocol - Demonstrated expertise in **diplomatic protocol** and relations with high-ranking officials from the PRC, Taiwan and Singapore.

Emerging Markets - Planned and executed strategy to expand focus throughout **emerging markets** worldwide.

Expatriate - Designed compensation and benefit programs for **expatriate** and foreign national employees in South Africa.

Export - Redesigned and streamlined logistics, warehousing and distribution operations to expand **export** programs throughout the European continent.

Feasibility Analysis - Conducted a complex, in-country **feasibility analysis** project to determine potential market and profitability for Latin American manufacturing.

Foreign Government Affairs - Built cooperative working relationships with officials to strengthen the organization's **foreign government affairs** practices and support cooperative initiatives.

Foreign Investment - Lobbied before state and federal legislatures to advance **foreign investment** opportunities in Central and South America.

Global Expansion - Challenged to plan and execute a large-scale **global expansion** and marketing initiative to transition Farm Bureau from a national to international organization.

Global Market Position - Evaluated competitive activity, competitive products, emerging technologies and new markets to determine the corporation's **global market position**.

Global Marketing - Recruited to plan and orchestrate IBM's **global marketing** and business development initiatives across five continents.

Global Sales - Recruited in-country sales teams and built/led a **global sales** organization that consistently exceeded revenue, profit and market share quotas.

Import - Redesigned internal documentation processes, expanded transportation programs and increased **import** revenues by more than 37% within first year.

Intellectual Property - Designed contracts, agreements and other legal documents to protect the corporation's **intellectual property** from unauthorized licensing and distribution.

International Business Development - Senior Marketing Executive with full strategic and tactical responsibility for leading the corporation's worldwide **international business development** programs.

International Business Protocol - Demonstrated proficiency in **international business protocol** across diverse cultures, economies and markets.

International Financing - Structured a three-party **international financing** agreement between Aramco, Bechtel and Caterpillar for $16 million development project in Saudi Arabia.

International Liaison - Trained new sales recruits in **international liaison**, marketing and business development skills.

International Licensee - Structured and negotiated Apple Computer's first-ever **international licensee** agreement for product marketing in Eastern Europe.

International Marketing - Drove Martin Marietta's **international marketing** projects throughout Asia and Latin America.

International Sales - Created a worldwide **international sales** organization through direct, VAR, reseller and mass merchant channels.

International Subsidiary - Established and managed **international subsidiary** to provide manufacturing, distribution, sales and marketing leadership for the entire PacRim region.

International Trade - Captured **international trade** opportunities worldwide and increased technology sales by more than 225% over four years.

Joint Venture - Negotiated a complex **joint venture** agreement for the development of a $8.2 million cement manufacturing plant in Thailand.

Licensing Agreements - Worked with corporate counsel to structure **licensing agreements** with distributors worldwide.

Local National - Designed recruitment, training, benefit and compensation systems for **local nationals**.

Market Entry - Spearheaded **market entry** into Brazil, negotiated $8.9 million in first year sales and outpaced the competition.

Marketing - Directed classical **marketing**, market research and strategic planning functions at corporate headquarters for six independent operating companies.

Merger - Facilitated **merger** and integration of all information technology, order processing, billing and product delivery programs for Time Warner's first international acquisition.

Multi-Channel Distribution Network - Designed organizational infrastructure and created a **multi-channel distribution network** to expand product reach throughout the reseller and retail markets.

Offshore Operations - Championed development of **offshore operations** to reduce labor and overhead costs associated with food products manufacturing.

Public/Private Partnership - Negotiated **public/private partnership** agreements between U.S. manufacturers and Australian government officials to introduce advanced telecommunications technologies.

Technology Licensing - Structured and executed complex **technology licensing** agreements between manufacturers and distributors throughout France, Germany and the U.K.

Start-Up Venture - Led **start-up venture** through planning, staffing and budgeting to full-scale operation within first 120 days.

Strategic Alliance - Negotiated **strategic alliance** with Motorola to develop joint technology and avionics programs.

Strategic Planning - Directed long-term **strategic planning** projects for 16 corporations working cooperatively to transition from domestic to global marketing/business development.

Technology Transfer - Identified opportunity to expand market penetration and led a series of sophisticated **technology transfer** programs throughout Europe, Asia and Africa.

PAUL MANDAU
49 Dawson Avenue
Albany, New York 10303-3556
Phone / Fax (914) 921-3245

SENIOR GENERAL MANAGEMENT / BUSINESS DEVELOPMENT
MARKETING & SALES MANAGEMENT
U.S., Europe, Latin America, Middle East, Far East & Africa

Strong executive career leading successful start-up, turnaround and fast-track growth marketing corporations worldwide. Combines expertise in business development, product positioning and market expansion with strong operating, financial, HR and manufacturing management record. Fluent in French and Spanish. Conversational in Portuguese, Arabic, Greek and Slovak. MBA Degree.

Contributed to significnat revenue/profit growth through decisive and proactive management. Specialist in start-ups, turnarounds and strategic alliances in emerging markets.

PROFESSIONAL EXPERIENCE:

PRINCETON COSMETICS, White Plains, New York   1995 to 1996

Director - International Business Development

Recruited to plan and orchestrate aggressive market development and business development initiatives throughout emerging markets worldwide for this $75 million corporation. Challenged to build new market presence while reengineering and expanding existing international sales and distribution operations. Authored strategic marketing plans, tactical sales and channel development initiatives. Led a team of sales/marketing managers.

- Built international sales revenues from $4 million to $7 million (75%). Projections indicate 115% growth over next 12 months.

- Identified and captured opportunities for explosive growth throughout the Pacific Rim. Negotiated strategic alliances with major distributors throughout Japan, China, Korea and the Philippines. Evaluated feasibility of and recommended joint venture in China.

- Structured and negotiated strategic alliance with South and West African business partners to expand presence within high-growth emerging markets.

- Revitalized sales, marketing and distribution operations throughout Mexico after four years of stagnant sales. Projections indicate 400% growth over next 12 months.

BRAND ONE, INC., White Plains, New York   1991 to 1994

General Manager - Latin America

Reversed six-year negative P&L performance of 16 distributor markets throughout Latin America. Designed and led sales, product and management training programs for 660 distributor sales, administrative and support personnel. Personally developed and managed relationships with major accounts throughout the region.

- Generated net sales increase of $1.2 million (295%), operating profit growth of $600,000 (36%) and market share improvement to 89%.

- Increased volume 253% through increased distribution and design/implementation of innovative category and market support programs.

SMITH & LEILSON DRUG, INC., New York, New York   1987 to 1990

Managing Director - Chile (1989 to 1990)

Full P&L, operating and business development responsibility for an independent subsidiary with 139 employees. Scope of responsibility included the entire manufacturing operation (staffing, budgeting, capital expenditures, production planning/scheduling, quality, safety), all financial and administration functions, and a high-profile sales and marketing organization.

- Reversed four year sales, operating profit and market share reduction. Grew sales to \$12 million (175%), operating profit to \$2.7 million (285%) and volume by 31%. Reduced cost of goods 19% and number of SKU's from 184 to 109.

- Recaptured market leadership in core OTC categories: analgesics (20%), antacids (23%), muscle relaxants (58%) and deodorants (21%).

Director - Latin American Business Development (1987 to 1988)

Revitalized Mexican and Brazilian sales/marketing organizations, initiated several successful new product introductions, and designed a series of existing product revitalizations on regional basis.

- Built sales to \$213 million (18% increase) and operating profits to \$15 million (105% increase) in a 27 subsidiary division.

PFIZER, INC., New York, New York   1967 to 1986

Rapid promotion through increasingly responsible offshore sales, marketing and new business development management positions. Career highlights included:

Associate Director - International Business Development (1985 to 1986)

Headquarters assignment with newly-formed senior management group established to develop and implement international business expansion opportunities. Directed start-up of Turkish joint venture (\$40 million in first year sales), expanded licensing agreements in Pakistan and Bangladesh, and converted West African importing operations to manufacturing subsidiaries.

Managing Director - Egypt (1981 to 1984)

Directed start-up of the first U.S. company to open direct operations in Egypt. Held full P&L responsibility for 24 manufacturing and administrative personnel, and a countrywide sales distribution network. Built revenues to \$2 million despite government-subsidized competition.

Business Development Director - Argentina (1980)

Closed non-performing joint venture in Chile and transitioned into a profitable trading company. Renegotiated licensing agreement in Haiti, and led negotiations for Argentine acquisition.

Marketing & Sales Director / New Products Director / Product Manager (1967 to 1979)

- Increased revenues in metropolitan France and French West Africa from under \$60 million in 1969 to \$200 million in 1974 through new product launches.

- Increased Colombian sales from \$60 million in 1977 to \$100+ million in 1979.

- Built revenues in Greece from \$6 million to \$25 million within two years.

EDUCATION: CALIFORNIA STATE UNIVERSITY
               MBA, International Business, 1966
               BS, Business Management, 1965

LAW & CORPORATE LEGAL AFFAIRS

Positions

Arbitrator

Associate

Associate Attorney

Associate Counselor

Attorney

Corporate Counselor

Corporate Secretary

Counselor

General Counsel

General Managing Partner

Paralegal

Lawyer

Legal Assistant

Legal Counsel

Managing Partner

Mediator

Partner

Senior Attorney

Senior Counsel

Senior Partner

Vice President of Corporate Law & Administration

KeyWords

Acquisition - Directed legal and contract negotiations for over $200 million in corporate,product and technology **acquisitions** during Tandem's rapid growth and global expansion.

Adjudicate - **Adjudicated** employee claims alleging harassment, unfair promotion and discriminatory hiring practices.

Administrative Law - Served as Westmoreland County's only **administrative law** judge for 10 consecutive years.

Antitrust - Successfully defended **antitrust** law suit brought by Apple alleging use of their proprietary technologies in Xerox's latest generation of laser printers.

Briefs - Wrote **briefs**, memoranda, petitions, correspondence, motions and other legal documentation for the firm's real estate practice.

Case Law - Researched **case law** in preparation of Iowa's first industrial espionage criminal case.

Client Management - In addition to all trial responsibilities, accountable for client development and **client management** with major corporations.

Contracts Law - Specialized in **contracts law** with particular emphasis on international trade, technology licensing and multinational joint ventures.

Copyright Law - Administered Random House's **copyright law**, infringement and litigation affairs.

Corporate By-Laws - Wrote **corporate by-laws** following the spin-off of Larabie's banking division to create a new corporation with new board of directors and new management team.

Corporate Law - Held full responsibility for the strategic planning and leadership of the entire **Corporate Law** Department, encompassing both domestic and international legal affairs.

Corporate Recordkeeping - Appointed Board Secretary responsible for **corporate recordkeeping**, shareholder communications and year-end reporting.

Criminal Law - Built and managed a successful **criminal law** practice specializing in the prosecution of repeat offenders.

Cross-Border Transactions - Negotiated **cross-border transactions** for the sale of IBM technology into emerging Mexican markets.

Depositions - Administered **depositions** for all legal proceedings conducted under the jurisdiction of the Montgomery County Circuit Court.

Discovery - Directed **discovery** in representation of alleged malpractice incident.

Due Diligence - Managed **due diligence** for all corporate mergers, acquisitions, joint ventures and strategic alliances worldwide.

Employment Law - Restructured **employment law** division to meet regulatory requirements and corporate policy for retention and promotion.

Environmental Law - Resolved complex **environmental law** issues arising from improper handling of hazardous waste and disposal.

Ethics - Created vision and established corporate **ethics** committee to advance community-based fundraising, support and services.

Family Law - Practiced **family law** with an emphasis on the placement and custody of minors.

Fraud - Investigated alleged incidents of **fraud** perpetrated by previous CFO during his 10-year tenure with the corporation.

General Partnership - Structured and transacted all legal contracts for the formation of a real estate **general partnership**.

Intellectual Property - Wrote corporate legal requirements, standards and use provisions for the transfer of **intellectual property** rights.

Interrogatory - Prepared formal written responses to over 400 **interrogatory** questions during initial discovery procedures.

Joint Venture - Formed **joint venture** between ABC and PBS for the funding, production and distribution of environmental programming.

Judicial Affairs - Mediated resolution in **judicial affairs** proceedings between two conflicting municipalities.

Juris Doctor (JD) - Award **Juris Doctor** degree in 1989 as #1 in 420-person graduating class.

Labor Law - Earned a nationwide reputation for expertise in **law labor**, labor negotiations and mediation.

Landmark Decision - Led legal team in **landmark decision** on corporate taxation passed down by the U.S. Supreme Court.

Legal Advocacy - Provided aggressive **legal advocacy** and representation to human service agencies throughout Minnesota.

Legal Research - Conducted extensive **legal research** and analysis to uncover relevant case law from the early 1930's.

Legislative Review/Analysis - Managed **legislative review/analysis** of changing regulations, identified impact on business operations and communicated reporting requirements to division vice presidents.

Licensing - Negotiated over $400 million in **licensing** and technology transfer agreements.

Limited Liability Corporation (LLC) - Established Bahamian-based **LLC** to protect real estate investment assets and sale proceeds.

Limited Partnership - Formed a **limited partnership** for the development of a 122-room resort in Grand Cayman.

Litigation - Personally managed all complex **litigation** arising from contractual disputes and non-performance.

Mediation - Directed successful **mediation** with union officials and averted potential work stoppage.

Memoranda - Wrote legal **memoranda** for submission to U.S. Claims Court disputing alleged non-compliance.

Mergers - Structured, negotiated and transacted six **mergers** in 1995 with total investment value of $44 million.

Motions - Drafted **motions** requesting several continuances in response to witness scheduling obligations.

Negotiations - Managed sensitive **negotiations** between plaintiffs and defendants to resolve issues prior to trial.

Patent Law - Specialized in **patent law** of industrial products, technologies and components.

Personal Injury - Refocused legal practice from family law to **personal injury** in response to changing client requirements for legal advice and representation.

Probate Law - Managed **probate law** of wills and estates with combined assets of more than $500 million.

Real Estate Law - Recruited to establish DYD's first-ever, in-house **Real Estate Law** Department to manage expanding real estate investment projects and control over $1 billion in assets.

Risk Management - Expanded corporate **risk management** program to include administration of all pension and 401(k) plans.

SEC Affairs - Administered this Wall Street investment firm's **SEC affairs**, reporting and compliance program.

Settlement Negotiations - Transacted disposition of $1 million in assets through **settlement negotiations** between family members and corporation.

Shareholder Relations - Designed and produced a portfolio of corporate communications to strengthen **shareholder relations** and restore credibility.

Signatory Authority - Held **signatory authority** for all corporate, financial and legal documents.

Strategic Alliance - Pioneered the corporation's first-ever **strategic alliance** with an emerging telecommunications service provider.

Tax Law - Directed local, state, federal and international **tax law** for IBM.

Technology Transfer - Negotiated over $340 million in **technology transfer** agreements with business partners in Mexico, Colombia and Brazil.

Trade Secrets - Devised strategy to protect the corporation's **trade secrets** following notification of an alleged industrial espionage ring.

Trademark - Revitalized the corporation's commitment to security and authored new **trademark** protection policy.

Transactions Law - Fast-track promotion throughout corporate legal career with an emphasis in domestic and international **transactions law**, contracts and intellectual property.

Trial Law - Maintained a 90%+ winning rate in all **trial law** proceedings.

Unfair Competition - Investigated and mediated alleged incidents of **unfair competition** in the aerospace and semiconductor industries.

Workers' Compensation Litigation - Successfully resolved 12 pending **workers' compensation litigation** cases to the satisfaction of both management and union officials.

WARREN T. COLLINS

39349 South Bay Street
San Francisco, California 96375
E-Mail: WTC225@mcimail.com

Home (415) 493-7459

Office (415) 246-5894

CORPORATE GENERAL COUNSEL

*Technology Licensing / Mergers & Acquisitions / Joint Ventures / Patents & Trademarks
Litigation & Claims Defense / Corporate Finance / Human Resource Affairs / Contracts*

PROFESSIONAL EXPERIENCE:

PFIZER, INC., Redwood Valley, California   1989 to Present
(Fortune 500 specialty pharmaceutical, medical device, surgical equipment and optical products manufacturer with over 20 major operating subsidiaries worldwide and 1996 revenues of $1.5 billion)

Associate General Counsel & Assistant Secretary (1989 to Present)
Regional General Counsel - Japan (1991 to Present)
Recruited back to previous employer as Senior Counsel responsible for worldwide intellectual property (IP) affairs and licensing, with an IP portfolio of 7500+ trademarks and 1500 patents. Direct a staff of 11 including five attorneys and three paralegals. Manage $5 million operating budget.

- Deputy to General Counsel for administration of Corporate Legal Department of 25 including 11 attorneys and six paralegals.
- Structure and negotiate licensing contracts with global pharmaceutical companies, biotechnology companies and universities for product acquisitions. Negotiate co-promotion, distribution and supply agreements worldwide.
- Direct all patent and trademark origination, enforcement and defense actions worldwide. Travel throughout Europe, Japan, Australia and North America.
- Provide legal consultation for merger, acquisition and joint venture transactions. Select and direct outside counsel worldwide.

Concurrent appointment as **Corporate Counsel** for Allergan's operations in Japan and as a **Board Member** for two Japanese subsidiaries. Directed all general legal affairs through a multinational legal team (e.g., IP, contracts, leases, joint ventures, employment agreements, claims and litigation).

NOTE: Accelerated number of patent awards through improved legal process. Ranked by IPO as one of the top 200 organizations worldwide in number of U.S. patents granted in 1996.

LEGAL & BUSINESS CONSULTANT, Golden City, California   1984 to 1989

Independent Consultant to CEOs, COOs, Presidents and Boards of Directors of emerging technology, pharmaceutical and consumer products industries. Provided expertise in patent law, portfolio valuation, technology valuation, regulatory affairs and new venture start-up.

- Retained for one-year interim assignment as **General Counsel** for Biomedics (biotech R&D venture) to guide the development of in-house legal and patent departments.
- Developed consulting relationship with the California Cancer Research Foundation regarding intellectual property, portfolio evaluation, patents and related legal actions/claims.
- Developed and obtained first FDA approval (ANDA) of a generic product for a widely-used branded surgical scrub for start-up company. Took venture through development and approval, thereafter negotiating successful sale.

WARREN T. COLLINS   *Page Two*

MERIWETHER RESEARCH & DEVELOPMENT COMPANY, San Jose, California   1981 to 1984

Executive Vice President, General Counsel, CFO & Secretary
Joined Meriwether Research to direct this drug development company's IPO following its spin-off from Allergan Pharmaceuticals. Raised $25 million and placed stock on NASDAQ (managed by Merrill Lynch). Achieved market capitalization of $250 million.

Held full accountability for all IP, general and corporate legal, financial, accounting and human resource affairs for the corporation. Managed a large out-licensing effort for drug development candidates and adjuncts, corporate financial and strategic planning, budgeting, contracts, joint venture and long-range corporate development functions. Directed a staff of 15.

- Patented and licensed CLEOCIN-T, FDA approved prescription antibiotic acne formulation. Product delivered $50+ million in annual revenues to licensee (Upjohn).
- Raised an additional $5 million in revenues through negotiation of strategic R&D partnerships with major multinational and regional pharmaceutical companies in Japan and Europe.

PFIZER , INC., Irvine, California   1973 to 1981

General Counsel - Allergan International Division (1977 to 1981)
Assistant General Counsel & Assistant Secretary (1975 to 1981)
Senior Legal Counsel directing Allergan's IP, corporate development, contracts, in-licensing and out-licensing programs worldwide. Spearheaded the start-up of new company subsidiaries, manufacturing operations and joint ventures in the U.K., France, Italy, Japan and Ireland.

Vice President & General Counsel - Nelson Research (1973 to 1975)
Directed corporate development, merger, acquisition, licensing, contracts and drug development programs worldwide. Guided top scientists in early stage development of computer-assisted drug design technologies. Directed the award of over 50 patents with numerous foreign corresponding patents and licenses.

EDUCATION: **JD (Honors)**, The George Washington University National Law Center
                     MBA, Pepperdine University School of Business and Management
                     BS (Chemistry), University of California at Berkeley

PROFESSIONAL ACTIVITIES:

Bar Admissions	State Bar of California, U.S. Patent and Trademark Office Bar, U.S. Supreme Court
Associations	American Intellectual Property Law Assn., Licensing Executives Society, American Corporate Patent Counsel, Editorial Board (Managing Intellectual Property)
Publications	Editorial Board Member & Contributing Writer to "Managing Intellectual Property," European-based monthly legal publication: — "Patent Practitioners - Don't Let GATT Get You," March 1995 (republished by IP section of California State Bar) — "Intellectual Property and Pharmaceuticals," Patent Yearbook, 1995
Presentations	Presentations sponsored by the Practicing Law Institute (PLI) in San Francisco, 1993, published by PLI in its "Global Intellectual Property Series": — "Patent Litigation in Civil Law Countries"; "Contact Lens Care Litigation"

MANUFACTURING & OPERATIONS MANAGEMENT

Positions

Assistant Manufacturing Manager

Assistant Operations Manager

Assistant Plant Manager

Assistant Production Manager

Director

Director of Manufacturing

Director of Operations

Distribution Manager

Engineering Manager

Facilities Manager

General Manager

Group Manager

Inventory Control Analyst

Inventory Control Manager

Logistics Manager

Manufacturing Associate

Manufacturing Engineer

Manufacturing Manager

Manufacturing Operations Manager

Materials Manager

Operations Manager

Operations Superintendent

Pilot Plant Manager

Plant Manager

Plant Superintendent

Process Manager

Product Line Manager

Production Control Manager

Production Manager

Production Supervisor

Project Manager

Quality Manager

Shift Supervisor

Vice President of Distribution

Vice President of Logistics

Vice President of Manufacturing

Vice President of Operations

Vice President of Production

KeyWords

Asset Management - Directed **asset management** functions for 20 manufacturing facilities, two distribution centers and 68 sales offices nationwide, with total asset value exceeding $2.1 billion.

Automated Manufacturing - Transitioned Playtex from a labor-intensive production operation into a state-of-the-art **automated manufacturing** facility.

Capacity Planning - Facilitated **capacity planning** to consolidate Canadian, Mexican and U.S. operations into one centralized production operation.

Capital Budget - Controlled a $280 million **capital budget** allocated for technology acquisition.

Capital Project - Brought Johnson's most significant **capital project** in the past 10 years from concept through planning, staffing and budgeting to full-scale operations and on-time completion.

Cell Manufacturing - Transitioned from traditional line production to **cell manufacturing**, delivering a 22% improvement in product quality and 35% gain in daily production yields.

Computer Integrated Manufacturing (CIM) - Spearheaded implementation of **CIM**, CAD, JIT and SPC systems/technologies to accelerate production output and strengthen quality performance.

Concurrent Engineering - Introduced **concurrent engineering** processes that significantly enhanced transition from R&D to prototype manufacture to full-scale production.

Continuous Improvement - Implemented **continuous improvement** processes and achieved a 24% gain in product quality ratings.

Cost Avoidance - Created environment that rewarded individual employees for contributions to long-term **cost avoidance** and profit growth.

Cost Reductions - Captured over $2 million in material **cost reductions** through expanded vendor sourcing.

Cross-Functional Teams - Championed development of **cross-functional teams** to address critical productivity, efficiency and quality issues negatively impacting production yields and customer satisfaction.

Cycle Time Reduction - Created formal production schedules, retrained supervisory staff and impacted a measurable program of **cycle time reduction**.

Distribution Management - Architected the corporation's first-ever nationwide **distribution management** and warehouse control program.

Efficiency Improvement - Guided **efficiency improvement** initiatives throughout all core production planning, production scheduling and manufacturing operations.

Environmental Health & Safety (EHS) - Forged strategic partnership with Human Resources to create a performance-driven **EHS** program for all 10 IBM manufacturing facilities in the Northeast.

Equipment Management - Designed **equipment management** protocols to divest obsolete technology and redeploy advanced equipment resources to high-growth product lines.

Ergonomically Efficient - Redesigned manufacturing plant and created **ergonomically efficient** workstations, reducing extended employee absences and saving over $250,000 in annual workers' compensation costs.

Facilities Consolidation - Advised Manufacturing Manager in design and implementation of a nationwide **facilities consolidation** program.

Inventory Control - Implemented **inventory control** models and processes which reduced   on-hand inventory assets by more than $3 million.

Inventory Planning - Launched a large-scale **inventory planning** function in cooperation with Emerson, 3M and AlliedSignal to control Joyner's annual inventory expenses.

Just-In-Time (JIT) - Modified Raytheon's **JIT** processes for implementation throughout all Motorola divisions, affiliates and subsidiaries.

Labor Efficiency - Improved **labor efficiency** ratings by 12% through in-house training and staff development efforts.

Labor Relations - Managed sensitive **labor relations** initiatives during 6-month union contract negotiations.

Logistics Management - Created an integrated **logistics management** program assimilating all purchasing, inventory, distribution and warehousing functions.

Manufacturing Engineering - Recruited to build and direct the corporation's **Manufacturing Engineering** Division in an aggressive effort to upgrade production facilities, processes and   technologies.

Manufacturing Integration - Coordinated **manufacturing integration** of five acquisitions into core production operations.

Manufacturing Technology - Acquired over $5 million in **manufacturing technology** and robotics to fully automate the entire production operation.

Master Schedule - Designed **master schedule** for annual and five-year manufacturing plans.

Materials Planning - Revised **materials planning** programs to incorporate six new product lines into all production and distribution sites nationwide.

Materials Replenishment System (MRP) - Introduced **MRP** II system to support start-up of ISO 9000 certification process.

Multi-Site Operations - Challenged to revitalize **multi-site operations**, reduce labor and material costs, upgrade quality performance and strengthen customer loyalty.

Occupational Health & Safety (OH&S) - Designed Layton's first **OH&S** program, achieving compliance with both state and federal regulations governing hazardous materials handling and transportation.

On-Time Delivery - Improved **on-time delivery** from 56% to 98% within first year.

Operating Budget - Challenged to reduce $8.7 million annual **operating budget** through facilities, staff and technology consolidation.

Operations Management - Senior **Operations Management** Executive with full P&L responsibility for six manufacturing plants and a staff of more than 2000.

Operations Reengineering - Orchestrated an aggressive **operations reengineering** initiative and delivered a 22% improvement in production output, 10% reduction in material costs and 34% improvement in key account retention.

Operations Start-Up - Recruited by CEO to plan and orchestrate **operations start-up** of clean room manufacturing facility.

Optimization - Worked to identify and implement methods to enhance **optimization** of production yields and finished product.

Order Fulfillment - Managed a 52-person **order fulfillment** operation supplying major customers in North America, Latin America, Europe and Asia.

Order Processing - Reengineered and upgraded **order processing** systems, achieving 99% same day delivery.

Outsourcing - Pioneered Lytec's first-ever assembly **outsourcing** operation and captured 12% reduction in labor costs over first six months.

Participative Management - Forged implementation of **participative management** strategies in cooperation with management teams, union officials and hourly union personnel.

Performance Improvement - Guided a series of **performance improvement** programs that transitioned LTR from #4 to #1 in the industry.

Physical Inventory - Eliminated the need for annual **physical inventory** inspections through introduction of JIT systems/processes.

Pilot Manufacturing - Introduced new electronic technology into **pilot manufacturing** plant prior to full-scale production.

Plant Operations - Challenged to revitalize **plant operations**, eliminate redundancy, automate repetitive functions and improve bottom-line profitability.

Process Automation - Led an aggressive **process automation** program that computerized 115 manual processes and virtually eliminated all documentation requirements.

Process Redesign/Reengineering - Spearheaded an aggressive **process redesign/reengineering** program that increased manufacturing yields by 22%, reduced staffing requirements by 35% and contributed to a 44% improvement in YTD profits.

Procurement - Revitalized **procurement** operations, introduced international sourcing to supplement domestic vendor programs, and controlled $245 million in annual purchasing contracts.

Product Development & Engineering - Assembled cross-functional project team challenged to re-invent Myer-Rand's complete **product development and engineering** organization.

Product Rationalization - Initiated a large-scale **product rationalization** process to identify top performers and eliminate non-producers.

Production Forecasting - Designed a PC-based model to accelerate **production forecasting** and planning processes.

Production Lead Time - Slashed **production lead times** by more than 60% following implementation of computerized planning and scheduling technologies.

Production Management - Recruited to revitalize **production management** competencies in a downtrending market and industry.

Production Plans/Schedules - Established bi-annual **production plans and schedules** in cooperation with plant managers and production supervisors nationwide.

Production Output - Recruited the industry's most notable troubleshooter, provided technical and labor resources, and supported his efforts in enhancing **production output**, product quality and cost savings.

Productivity Improvement - Credited with a 34% gain in **productivity improvement** and product reliability.

Profit & Loss (P&L) Management - Senior Manufacturing Executive with full **P&L management** responsibility for the strategic planning, staffing, assets and field operations of Raydoc's entire manufacturing organization.

Project Budget - Allocated $2 million **project budget** to renovate warehousing and distribution facilities throughout Ohio.

Purchasing Management - Redesigned **purchasing management** and contracting processes for a net $2 million annual cost savings.

Quality Assurance/Quality Control - Devised and implemented an integrated **quality assurance/quality control** process that improved finished product quality ratings by more than 30%.

Quality Circles - Led six **quality circles** challenged to eliminate obstacles to quality control and improve overall performance of operations, products and components.

Regulatory Compliance - Achieved/surpassed all **regulatory compliance** standards as per OSHA, FDA, DOT, and other state and federal agencies.

Safety Management - Architected the corporation's first-ever **safety management** program and delivered a 24% reduction in lost time accidents over first two years.

Safety Training - Developed curriculum, trained instructors and supervised a plant-wide **safety training** program.

Shipping & Receiving Operation - Restructured business processes to create a performance-driven, customer-driven **shipping and receiving operation**.

Spares & Repairs Management - Established in-house s**pares and repairs management** function to reduce reliance on, and costs associated with, third party vendors.

Statistical Process Control (SPC) - Implemented **SPC** into all core design, engineering and manufacturing operations.

Technology Integration - Spearheaded $2.8 million **technology integration** project into Gryner's German and French manufacturing operations.

Time & Motion Studies - Conducted a series of **time and motion studies** that identified and virtually eliminated all production inefficiencies.

Total Quality Management (TQM) - Credited with the design and implementation of a fully-integrated **TQM** program that positioned TerraLand as #1 in timbering operations.

Traffic Management - Created a global **traffic management** function to coordinate product distribution throughout Europe, Asia and emerging African nations.

Turnaround Management - Challenged to plan and orchestrate an aggressive **turnaround management** initiative to transition Xylog from loss to sustained profitability despite intense market competition.

Union Negotiations - Participated in strategy planning and consensus building for favorable **union negotiations**.

Value-Added Processes - Implemented **value-added processes** to support Frester's global acquisition and operations integration programs.

Vendor Management - Structured a sophisticated **vendor management** program with measurable quality, productivity and efficiency objectives.

Warehousing Operations - Redesigned **warehousing operations**, reduced staffing requirements 12% and improved net profitability 28%.

Work in Progress (WIP) - Reduced **WIP** by 30% through introduction of cellular manufacturing and robotics technology.

Workflow Optimization - Engineered **workflow optimization** processes for a 34% improvement in daily production output.

Workforce Management - Credited with the creative design and integration of innovative **workforce management**, motivation and incentive programs.

World Class Manufacturing (WCM) - Transitioned HGM Computers from a small technology venture into a **world class manufacturing** operation recognized as one of Fortune's 100 fastest growing enterprises.

Yield Improvement - Introduced improved production processes and delivered 22% gain in **yield improvement**.

LEWIS L. LAYNE
P.O. Box 3359
Marion, Illinois 60345-3359
(847) 278-8712

SENIOR MANAGEMENT EXECUTIVE
Global Manufacturing / Multi-Site Plant Operations / Industrial Engineering

Talented Management Executive with 20 years of experience building and leading manufacturing operations throughout the U.S. and abroad. Recognized as a subject matter expert on facilitating process change and implementation through training, direction and motivation of operating staff and management teams.

• Strategic Business Planning & Reengineering	• Quality & Performance Improvement
• Cost Containment & Profit Growth	• Inventory & Supply Chain Management
• Management of Technology	• Production Processes & Controls

PROFESSIONAL EXPERIENCE:

LAYNE & ASSOCIATES, Marion, Illinois   1994 to Present

Managing Partner

Founded an exclusive consulting practice working with leading firms to provide expertise in manufacturing operations, supply chain management and management of technology. Lead cross-functional project teams in the analysis, redesign and implementation of operating enhancements to create world class manufacturing organizations. Key projects and highlights include:

• *Petrochemical Operation, Bombay, India*. Led the assessment of the reliability performance of a world-scale petrochemicals operation. Focused efforts on performance improvement processes and the maintenance, stroreroom and purchasing functions. Proposed reorganization and establishment of controls to improve reliability. **RESULTS**: Identified $25 million profit improvement and increased plant throughput by 12%.

• *Diesel Engine Manufacturer, Cape Town, South Africa*. Contracted for a 7-month on-site assignment to improve production planning and inventory control functions for the leading diesel engine manufacturer in Africa. **RESULTS**: Implemented a plan-do-review process with team centers and key performance indicators. Increased customer service levels from 70% to 95% and reduced inventories from 77 to 45 days on-hand.

• *Kellogg Graduate School/Northwestern University, Chicago, Illinois*. While completing Masters program, participated in management of technology research project sponsored by General Motors, Kodak and Rockwell International. **RESULTS**: Developed process based model for management of technology. Conducted high-level evaluations of existing management of technology processes and identified potential best practices for use throughout industry.

ALEXANDER & ALEXANDER   1988 to 1994

Management Consultant

Recruited to join this global consulting group based on expertise in the design and delivery of value-added process improvements for major Fortune 500 and international corporations. Managed the complete project cycle including client assessment, engagement planning, proposal development and project delivery. Key clients included Johnson & Johnson, Mobil Oil, Dole Foods, Ford, Kraft/General Foods, Procter & Gamble, and Merck Pharmaceuticals.

LEWIS L. LAYNE - Page Two

- Identified potential $55 million cost savings for General Motors through manufacturing benchmarking throughout the Saginaw Steering Systems Division.
- Spearheaded the design/implementation of a comprehensive maintenance planning and scheduling process for Dole Foods. Reduced manpower by 40% within seven months.
- Assessed and redesigned work processes throughout Novacor's maintenance planning and scheduling department. Reduced work backlogs by 80%.
- Facilitated the consolidation of Golden Cat's multi-site operations from four distinct facilities into three as part of a corporate-wide capacity and consolidation analysis.

REESE LABORATORIES   1977 to 1988

Progressed through several increasingly responsible engineering and plant management assignments with this $12 billion mulitnational healthcare products supplier. Promoted based upon consistent success in operations management, cost control and business process reengineering.

Plant Engineering Section Head - Corporate Headquarters (1983 to 1988)

Operations Supervisor for biohazardous, pharmaceutical and clean room environmental systems of a 2.5 million sq.ft. complex of 40 buildings. Led team of 14 engineers and technical suport personnel responsible for environmental systems maintenance and operation. Challenged to establish group and develop procedures for new and existing facilities to meet environmental standards.

- Managed the installation of state-of-the-art automated facilities management system. Facilitated the start-up of one million sq.ft. of new operations.
- Reduced operating costs by $300,000 through efficient operation of environmental systems.

International Manufacturing Engineer (1979 to 1983)

Promoted to the $4 billion International Manufacturing Division. Implemented a cost reduction program for 35 manufacturing plants including program design, measurement, reporting of results and training. Led the assessment of 10 manufacturing facilities worldwide. Reduced operating expenses by $2 million annually. Received Presidential Award for outstanding performance.

Engineering Management Trainee (1977 to 1979)

Selected from a competitive group of candidates for a two-year management training program while completing Masters Degree. Completed four assignments within the Corporate Engineering Division including the utilities, projects, design and maintenance departments.

EDUCATION & CERTIFICATIONS:

M.S., Industrial Engineering, THE UNIVERSITY OF CHICAGO, 1997
Major: Operations Research; Minor: Management of Technology
M.B.A., NORTHWESTERN UNIVERSITY, 1987
Major: Finance; Minor: Marketing
M.S., Mechanical Engineering, NORTHWESTERN UNIVERSITY, 1980
B.S., Mechanical Engineering, THE UNIVERSITY OF CHICAGO, 1976

Certified in Production & Inventory Management, APICS
Certified Management Consultant, IMC
Registered Professional Engineer, Illinois

PUBLIC RELATIONS & CORPORATE COMMUNICATIONS

Positions

Advertising Director

Advertising Manager

Communications Director

Community Relations Manager

Conference Manager

Corporate Communications Specialist

Creative Director

Director of Corporate Communications

Editor

Events Manager

Legislative Affairs Director

Lobbyist

Managing Director of Corporate Communications

Marketing Associate

Marketing Manager

Media Relations Director

Meetings Manager

Political Affairs Director

Promotions Director

Press Director

Public Affairs Director

Public Affairs Officer

Public Relations Director

Special Events Director

Trade Show Manager

Vice President of Advertising

Vice President of Communications

Vice President of Creative Services

Writer

KeyWords

Advertising Communications - Designed, wrote and produced a complete portfolio of print and multimedia **advertising communications** for key corporate clients (e.g., Exxon, Johnson & Johnson, Sears, Neiman-Marcus, Lazarus).

Agency Relations - Directed **agency relations** with major advertising, marketing, direct mail and print production companies.

Brand Management - Full P&L responsibility for **brand management** of Baxter's #1 global product line ($340 million Xytol brand).

Brand Strategy - Refocused **brand strategy** to meet changing consumer demographics and buying preferences.

Broadcast Media - Established proactive working relations with major **broadcast media** to favorably manage press communications during major corporate downsizing.

Campaign Management - Brand Manager with full responsibility for **campaign management** and execution for nationwide market launch of Tide Extra, now a $400 million product line ranked #2 in market share.

Community Affairs - Partnered with community leaders in support of high-profile **community affairs**, revitalization and funding activities.

Competitive Market Lead - Revitalized Palmolive Liquid Soap product line and captured a strong and sustainable **competitive market lead**.

Community Outreach - Expanded regional healthcare advertising programs to include direct **community outreach** and community teaching programs.

Conference Planning - Guided **conference planning** and special event programs with full responsibility for logistics, menus, guest speakers, agendas, facilities and on-site security.

Cooperative Advertising - Negotiated **cooperative advertising** partnerships with major retailers and captured a 15% reduction in annual print and broadcast costs.

Corporate Communications - Spearheaded the design, development and production of a series of high-profile **corporate communications** to create the company's first fully-integrated corporate identity.

Corporate Identity - Designed logos, letterheads, home pages, videos and customer communications with a consistent and recognizable **corporate identity**.

Corporate Sponsorship - Identified market opportunity and negotiated a $2 million **corporate sponsorship** with Atlanta Allied Resources to fund Bill Tuttle's NASCAR racing team.

Corporate Vision - Defined new **corporate vision** and authored business plan incorporating critical organizational development, process reengineering and change management programs.

Creative Services - Selected suppliers and negotiated third-party **creative services** contracts for graphics design, copyrighting, photographic and print production services.

Crisis Communications - Managed sensitive **crisis communications** with major media worldwide.

Customer Communications - Won a 1992 industry award for "creative excellence" in design of outbound **customer communications** campaign.

Direct Mail Campaign - Wrote copy and coordinated production/mailing of 20,000-piece **direct mail campaign** to existing customer base that delivered $750,000 in repeat sales.

Electronic Advertising - Pioneered Mattel's launch into emerging **electronic advertising** and communications technologies.

Electronic Media - Integrated **electronic media** with traditional print promotions to expand corporate advertising and communications campaigns throughout emerging markets.

Employee Communications - Created a proactive **employee communications** campaign to link management expectations with employee incentives and performance goals.

Event Management - Directed site selection, budgeting, entertainment and on-site **event management** functions for over 200 meetings, conferences, training symposia and social programs annually.

Fundraising - Achieved/surpassed all **fundraising** objectives and delivered $2 million in donations to the American Red Cross.

Government Relations - Directed **government relations** program critical to the success and continued funding of advanced telecommunications R&D projects.

Grassroots Campaign - Won support of local advocacy group and spearheaded **grassroots campaign** successful in defeating proposed legislation.

Investor Communications - Created a high-impact, high-profile **investor communications** program that restored Apple's credibility throughout the Wall Street community.

Issues Management - Counseled President and CEO on critical **issues management** and response to media inquiries.

Legislative Affairs - Orchestrated **legislative affairs** programs in cooperation with local, state and federal legislators to support the passage of the 1990 Free Commerce Act.

Logistics - Led 16-person special events team responsible for all **logistics**, including travel, lodging, local transportation, meals and conference agenda.

Management Communications - Designed monthly **management communications** program to update all supervisory and management personnel on changing regulatory requirements and documentation procedures.

Market Research - Conducted nationwide competitive **market research** to drive strategy for next generation products.

Marketing Communications - Designed and produced all corporate **marketing communications**, advertisements, promotions, incentives, POS displays and home pages.

Media Buys - Directed **media buys** for over $2 billion in annual television advertising.

Media Placement - Negotiated front page **media placement** with *Forbes, Fortune* and *Time.*

Media Relations - Maintained positive **media relations** despite widespread coverage of environmental pollutants and leakage incidents.

Media Scheduling - Coordinated **media scheduling** in cooperation with new product roll-out team to accelerate new launch and distribution.

Meeting Planning - Directed **meeting planning** for training and leadership development programs for the Center for Creative Leadership.

Merchandising - Designed award-winning consumer products **merchandising** programs that contributed substantially to Macy's 20% sales gain in 1996.

Multimedia Advertising - Produced **multimedia advertising** and customer communications programs to more competitively position Lerner against emerging suppliers.

Political Action Committee (PAC) - Led GE's political action committee over a 10-year period, significantly improving the corporation's ability to influence favorable legislation.

Premiums - Designed **premiums** as a direct competitive incentive against mature product brands.

Press Releases - Wrote corporate **press releases** for distribution to all major print and broadcast media throughout North America, Latin America and Europe.

Print Media - Launched a new **print media** campaign that provided Sears with competitive market and price distinction.

Promotions - Developed POS **promotions** that increased Coke's sales in all regional WalMart locations by an average of 12% over six months.

Public Affairs - Challenged to restore regulatory confidence with a proactive **public affairs** and communications program.

Public Relations - Dominated the market with successful **public relations** initiatives targeted to major manufacturers, distributors, vendors, resellers and mass merchants.

Public Speaking - Managed **public speaking** engagements before investors, bankers, shareholders and directors to support further investment in emerging healthcare products.

Publications - Directed in-house writing team that delivered 35 technical, marketing and employee **publications** in 1996.

Publicity - Won major media **publicity** with the donation of $2 million to the National Gallery of Art.

Sales Incentives - Created performance-driven **sales incentives** to drive field teams to a better than 35% increase over last year's sales numbers.

Shareholder Communications - Revitalized **shareholder communications** program and restored credibility despite poor market and revenue performance.

Special Events - Planned, staffed, budgeted, advertised and managed **special events** nationwide to raise money for local AIDS charities and healthcare research programs.

Strategic Communications Plan - Authored the corporation's first-ever **strategic communications plan**, defined corporate vision and charted course of action over next five years.

Strategic Planning - Member of 6-person senior executive team responsible for annual **strategic planning**, business development and market expansion.

Strategic Positioning - Elevated Midol's ranking in the HBA products industry through **strategic positioning** and product redefinition.

Tactical Campaign - Guided field sales, marketing and support teams in the implementation of **tactical campaigns** designed to accelerate profitable revenue growth.

Trade Shows - Represented emerging technology ventures at Comdex and other industry **trade shows** nationwide.

VIP Relations - Launched a high-profile and successful **VIP relations** program to strengthen partnerships with major corporate, industrial, government and not-for-profit clients.

REBECCA L. CORCORAN

210 East Chestnut Hill
Philadelphia, PA 19831
Home (215) 862-9724
Office (215) 831-8030

MARKETING / MEDIA & PUBLIC RELATIONS / SPECIAL EVENTS / SPORTING EVENTS
Creating High-Impact Images, Concepts, Services, Programs & Opportunities
To Build Revenues, Corporate Sponsorships and Fund Raising Contributions

Dynamic management career leading the conceptualization, creative design, planning, staffing, budgeting and promotion of successful marketing and special event programs worldwide. Expert in identifying market demand and building sustainable market presence. Skilled strategic planner, business manager, and sales/marketing director. Strong organizational, communication, public speaking and negotiations qualifications. Conversational French.

PROFESSIONAL EXPERIENCE:

Senior Associate   1991 to Present
THE POLETTI GROUP, Philadelphia, PA

Invited to join an elite real estate sales organization specializing in the marketing and sale of high-end residential properties throughout metropolitan New York.

- Achieved Million Dollar Roundtable each year. Promoted to Senior Associate after first year.
- Closed over $5 million in transactions within first five months of 1995. Ranked as one of the top sales producers in the organization.

Concurrent with The Poletti Group, chaired/co-chaired a series of high-profile fundraising and special event programs nationwide:

- Co-chaired the 1997 **Hot Springs Hospital Charity Luncheon**, one of the largest and most widely-covered events in the region. Increased fundraising by 25%. Selected to co-chair the 1998 event.
- Chaired the 1996 campaign for **Science Service**, a widely-publicized event launched to increase awareness of the innovative science scholarship and academic opportunities for young teenage candidates sponsored by the organization. Created a series of dynamic marketing and public relations materials to increase market visibility. Worked collaboratively with Honorary Chairperson Joan Rivers.
- Co-chaired the **Annual Red Cross Ball** (1990 to 1995), a prominent social event with celebrity sponsors including Deirdre Hall, Marla Maples and Mary Lou Whitney. Increased attendance from 250 in 1990 to 800+ in 1995 with Fortune 500 corporate sponsors.

Special Events Director   1990 to 1991
LONDON DOWNS POLO & COUNTRY CLUB, London Downs, NY

High-profile management position directing integrated marketing, special events, media and promotions programs for the Club, the Polo Museum and internationally-sponsored sporting events. Concurrent responsibility for spearheading national and international real estate sales and marketing programs for Equestrian Estates (high-end residential sub-community). Ranked as the #1 revenue producer.

- Appointed to the International Advisory Board for the Polo Museum. Personally launched a series of highly-successful fundraising and corporate sponsorship campaigns.
- Organized and executed an 800-person grand opening celebration with national and international media coverage.

Vice President of Marketing & Development   1988 to 1989
SILVER SERVICES, INC., Memphis, TN

Recruited to provide the direction, energy, strategy and expertise to launch an integrated sales, marketing and business development campaign for this retirement community corporation seeking to expand nationally. Authored first strategic marketing plan, directed $500,000 marketing and property development budget, and created a distinctive lifestyle community.

- Drove revenue growth by 20% within less than one year.

Regional Director of Marketing & Sales   1985 to 1988
NATIONAL RETIREMENT FOUNDATION, Memphis, TN

Fast-track promotion from Marketing Director to Marketing Director/Executive Director of a 175-unit, 20-acre upscale retirement community. Directed a staff of 54 and a $2.3 million annual operating budget. Created and successfully marketed a unique lifestyle and community culture that competitively positioned the property within the market and served as the corporate model for new project development. Promoted to Regional Director of Marketing & Sales (first in the history of the corporation) and given full responsibility for strategic planning, design and management of all new business development, advertising, public relations, special events and revenue generating programs for 12-14 projects nationwide.

- Led team that closed over $15.9 million in sales revenues in 1988.
- Maintained a high-profile position within the corporation. Led presentations to corporate investors, spoke at industry conferences and symposia, and directly managed press relations.

Co-Owner / General Manager   1974 to 1985
GRAY TRAVEL AGENCY, Memphis, TN

Co-founded a specialty travel and tour company with market focus on major specialty and sporting events worldwide (e.g., Melbourne Cup, The Olympics, World Championships). Designed unique tour packages for corporate clients, groups and associations. Personally managed daily agency operations, staffing, sales/marketing, customer service and contract negotiations. Built business to $2 million in annual sales.

PROFESSIONAL ACTIVITIES & AFFILIATIONS:

- **Independent Consultant** retained by Gross & Co. (1994 to Present), a newly-formed investment banking firm in Atlanta, Georgia, to provide expertise in **investor solicitation and negotiations** for a new $42 million fund (limited partnership with 6 high-profile board members including Norman Schwartzkoff). Travelled with partners to Europe to meet with potential investors in April 1995. Currently creating a portfolio of marketing and business development materials.

- **Special Events & Tour Consultant** with Elite Travel Services in Palm Beach, Florida (1994 to Present). Currently developing and marketing several unique travel packages to upscale resorts, sporting events and fundraising events worldwide (e.g., Princess Grace Foundation, Monte Carlo July 4th).

- **Founding Board Member of Equestrian Events, Inc.** , a non-profit organization formed by the Governor of the Tennessee in cooperation with the Tennessee Horse Park. Launched high-profile special events, fundraising programs and corporate sponsorships for the prestigious events. Served as President for two terms, Vice President for two terms and Secretary for two terms. Built fundraising budget from $1,500 to $450,000 over eight years.

EDUCATION: **BA Degree**, Speech & Hearing Pathology / Graduate Studies
                      UNIVERSITY OF KENTUCKY, Lexington, Kentucky

PURCHASING & LOGISTICS

Positions

Buyer
Certified Purchasing Manager (CPM)
Contracts Administrator
Contracts Manager
Corporate Purchasing Director
Director of Acquisitions
Director of Purchasing
Field Purchasing Manager
Logistics Manager
Materials Analyst
Materials Manager
Purchasing Agent
Purchasing Director
Purchasing Manager
Senior Buyer
Senior Product Analyst
Supplier Manager
Supply Manager
Vendor Relations Manager
Vice President of Materials & Resources
Vice President of Purchasing

KeyWords

Acquisition Management - Staffed and directed an **acquisition management** function responsible for over $2 billion in annual expenditures.

Barter Trade - Pioneered the development of an international **barter trade** program with Asian and European business partners to reduce domestic tax liabilities.

Bid Review - Managed a complex RFP and **bid review** process for the award of a $100 million healthcare research grant.

Buy vs. Lease Analysis - Developed PC-based models to enhance **buy vs. lease analysis** competencies.

Capital Equipment Acquisition - Directed over $50 million in **capital equipment acquisitions** during first year of $2 billion economic development program.

Commodities Purchasing - Managed a 12-person **commodities purchasing** business group responsible for electronics components acquisition in Japan, Korea and the Philippines.

Competitive Bidding - Administered the entire **competitive bidding** and contract award process for the $2 billion renovation of the New York Harbor Tunnel.

Contract Administration - Directed **contract administration**, negotiation and rebid functions for over $200 million in annual subcontracts.

Contract Change Order - Issued **contract change orders** to reflect design and engineering modifications.

Contract Negotiations - Led cross-functional teams responsible for all corporate **contract negotiations** for real estate acquisition and site development.

Contract Terms & Conditions - Standardized routine **contract terms and conditions** for all consumer lending relationships.

Cradle-To-Grave Procurement - Managed worldwide **cradle-to-grave procurement** contracts for the U.S. Army Materiel Command.

Distribution Management - Created a multi-channel **distribution management** program in cooperation with VARs, resellers, systems integrators and major consulting firms.

Economic Ordering Quantity Methodology - Introduced **economic ordering quantity methodolog**y, EVA principles and other sophisticated financial tools for purchasing, warehousing, inventory and distribution.

Fixed Price Contracts - Administered **fixed price contracts** with the U.S. Army, U.S. Navy, IBM, Xerox and Raytheon totalling over $40 million annually for the delivery of advanced navigational devices.

Indefinite Price/Indefinite Quantity - Managed **indefinite price/indefinite quantity** contracts for technology, communications, electronics and underwater surveillance systems.

International Sourcing - Introduced **international sourcing** and partnered with Asian manufacturers to market the first-ever RBR devices in the U.S.

International Trade - Expanded **international trade** into emerging African markets to capitalize upon acquisition and divestiture opportunities in various mineral commodities.

Inventory Planning/Control - Re-invented Fram's **inventory planning and control** function, introduced JIT principles, streamlined documentation requirements and cut inventory costs by 20% annually.

Just-in-Time (JIT) Purchasing - Successfully implemented **JIT purchasing** into 200 IBM manufacturing sites worldwide, resulting in a better than 5% reduction in annual purchasing and inventory holding costs.

Logistics Management - Created a fully-integrated **logistics management** function consolidating purchasing, inventory, warehousing and distribution.

Materials Management - Established a formal **materials management** function to gain control of parts, inventory, spares and WIP throughout 100,000 sq. ft. manufacturing plant.

Materials Replenishment Ordering (MRO) Purchasing - Introduced a series of productivity improvement programs including **MRO purchasing**, quality councils and an aggressive cost reduction initiative.

Multi-Site Operations - Planned, staffed, budgeted and directed all purchasing and contract functions for **multi-site operations** throughout Pennsylvania, Maryland and New Jersey.

Negotiation - Demonstrated powerful **negotiation** skills in challenging situations.

Offshore Purchasing - Reduced annual costs by $22 million through introduction of **offshore purchasing** and vendor partnerships.

Outsourced - Pioneered Kelly's successful transition from in-house to **outsourced** telecommunications and telemarketing services.

Price Negotiations - Managed sensitive **price negotiations** during $2 billion acquisition of American Savings Bank by Maryland National Bank.

Procurement - Appointed Project Officer responsible for worldwide **procurement** of military armament and explosives.

Proposal Review - Led team responsible for **proposal review**, cost analysis and evaluation for acquisition of $275 million avionics system.

Purchasing - Recruited to this emerging Internet venture to guide the development of a corporate **purchasing**, materials management, warehousing and data delivery function.

Regulatory Compliance - Directed **regulatory compliance** functions encompassing FAR, DFAR and state regulatory requirements.

Request for Proposal (RFP) - Issued 200+ **RFPs** in support of Syntex's $300 million nuclear plant expansion and retrofit.

Request for Quotation (RFQ) - Reviewed all **RFQ** submissions for $20 million healthcare services contract.

Sourcing - Expanded materials **sourcing** programs to include minority vendors in certified business districts.

Specifications Compliance - Reviewed contractor progress reports to ensure **specifications compliance** and accurate documentation.

Subcontractor Negotiations - Authorized general contractor to manage and administer all **subcontractor negotiations**.

Supplier Management - Created an integrated **supplier management** model based on partnership strategies and common visions.

Supplier Quality - Introduced a comprehensive **supplier quality** review and assessment process to strengthen quality of final consumer products.

Vendor Partnerships - Spearheaded profitable **vendor partnerships** to exploit common customer relationships and facilitate market expansion.

Vendor Quality Certification - Established a multi-year **vendor quality certification** program that contributed to a 22% increase in customer satisfaction/retention.

Warehousing - Managed a 22-site **warehousing** and product distribution organization to record performance, efficiency and profit levels.

WENDELL T. HOLMES
3984 SW Shore Drive
Tampa, Florida 33598
(897) 314-5431

CAREER SUMMARY:

Over 15 years experience managing high-volume **PURCHASING / MATERIALS MANAGEMENT / INVEN-TORY CONTROL** operations. Qualifications include:

- Purchasing Department Management
- Staffing/Training/Supervision
- Quality/Productivity Improvement
- Inventory Planning/Forecasting

- Vendor Sourcing/Selection
- Contract Negotiations/Administration
- Competitive Bidding/Award
- Cost Reduction/Avoidance

Certified Purchasing Manager (CPM) Candidate.

PROFESSIONAL EXPERIENCE:

PREMIERE MANUFACTURING, INC., Tampa, Florida   1994 to Present

Senior Purchasing Agent

Recruited by previous employer (automotive components manufacturer) for a senior-level position at the corporation's world headquarters. Scope of responsibility includes global vendor sourcing, vendor contract negotiations, materials planning and inventory analysis. Focus efforts on reducing net purchasing costs and lowering inventory volumes while maintaining adequate stock on hand to meet daily production flow.

GTE TELEPHONE COMPANY, Orion, Ohio   1990 to 1994

Purchasing Manager - Florida

Senior Purchasing Manager with full responsibility for planning, staffing, budgeting, and directing the entire purchasing organization for the company's operations throughout the state of Florida. Supervised a staff of eight direct reports and 27 indirect personnel. Total annual purchasing exceeded $100 million.

- Managed operations during a period of significant growth (e.g., purchase orders increased from 12,000 to 40,000 annually, line items increased from 4000 to 110,000).

- Realigned workforce of the Purchasing Department, reduced non-management staffing from 35 to 22 personnel, and saved the corporation $400,000 in annual payroll expenses.

- Established and staffed materials forecasting department to more effectively manage materials planning functions for company operations throughout the Southeast.

- Led design and implementation of a paperless purchasing and invoicing system that significantly upgraded the productivity, efficiency and quality of the entire materials management organization.

- Saved $75,000 in annual office supply and material costs through aggressive vendor negotiations.

- Managed telephone refurbishing and scrap disposal contract projected to save $1 million annually.

- Negotiated development and subsequent administration of a cooperative educational program with Tampa Technical Institute for start-up of a CPM Certification Program for GTE personnel.

WENDELL T. HOLMES - Page Two

PREMIERE MANUFACTURING, INC., Lexington, Virginia   1987 to 1990

Purchasing Agent

Scheduled and purchased all materials for press switch, solenoid, mini-pressure transducers and molding department (e.g., stampings, metals, copper, brass, stainless steel, screw machine components, molded parts, tooling). Responsible for vendor research, sourcing, bidding and documentation. Coordinated JIT purchasing averaging $1.7 million annually.

- Reduced R&D purchasing costs by $200,000 for one specific project (20% under projected costs).

- Saved $150,000 in costs on plastic components through negotiation of bulk purchasing agreements.

- Lowered product inventories by more than 25% annually ($250,000 estimated savings).

MELLON SYSTEMS, INC., Melbourne, Florida   1986 to 1987

Senior Buyer

Fast-paced purchasing, vendor sourcing and materials management position buying a diversity of commodities (e.g.,. primary electro/electromechanical products and metal fabricated materials, cabinetry, plant equipment, maintenance/repair supplies). Purchased for both the manufacturing and land/building divisions of the company. Held concurrent responsibility for research, selection and contracting with technical service consultants.

STEWART OFFICE SUPPLY, Ft. Myers, Florida   1985 to 1986

Sales Representative

Sold/marketed office equipment, furniture and supplies to commercial, industrial, and institutional accounts throughout the region. Met with prospective clients to evaluate product requirements, led presentations, negotiated pricing and closed final sales. Consistently met monthly quotas for sales revenues and new account development.

GTE TELEPHONE, Orion, Ohio   1973 to 1985

Purchasing Supervisor

Fast-track promotion through a series of increasingly responsible purchasing and warehouse management positions. Final assignment as Purchasing Supervisor included direct responsibility for training/supervising a staff of six in Materials Repair/Return.

EDUCATION:

TAMPA TECHNICAL INSTITUTE
30 credit hours toward CPM Certification

NATIONAL MANAGEMENT ASSOCIATION
Management Training & Supervisory Development Courses

REAL ESTATE, CONSTRUCTION & PROPERTY MANAGEMENT

Positions

Acquisition Director

Asset Manager

Broker of Record

Certified Property Manager (CPM)

Chief Executive Officer (CEO)

Chief Operating Officer (COO)

Director of Operations

Director of Property Management

Facilities Director

General Contractor

Leasing Director

Managing General Partner

Managing Partner

Partner

Portfolio Administrator

Portfolio Manager

President

Project Manager

Project Superintendent

Property Manager

Real Estate Developer

Real Estate Director

Real Estate Sales & Marketing Manager

Real Property Administrator (RPA)

Registered Property Manager (RPM)

Sales Associate

Vice President of Development

Vice President of Property Acquisition & Management

Vice President of Real Estate

KeyWords

Acquisition - Negotiated the **acquisition** of $200 million in investment property as part of Austin's downtown revitalization and economic development project.

American Disabilities Act (ADA) - Rewrote procedures for Building & Construction Division to incorporate recent **ADA** regulations for accessibility.

Asset Management - Responsible for **asset management** and disposition of over $2 billion in both commercial and multi-unit residential property.

Asset Valuation - Directed **asset valuation** of all proposed acquisitions, reviewed tenant leases and made final purchase recommendations.

Asset Workout/Recovery - Led **asset workout** teams in recovering over $200 million in distressed real estate assets.

Building Code Compliance - Directed on-site inspection of all completed new construction projects to ensure **building code compliance**.

Building Trades - Supervised over 200 subcontractors representing on all **building trades** during the construction of the $200 million Ivory Towers Project.

Capital Improvement - Planned, designed, budgeted and directed $189 million in facilities renovation and **capital improvement** projects.

Claims Administration - Simplified a complex **claims administration** and reporting process, streamlined documentation requirements and expedited funds disbursement.

Commercial Development - Managed over $500 million in **commercial development** projects including Class A office buildings, retail centers and retirement communities.

Community Development - Appointed to gubernatorial committee responsible for guiding policy governing **community development** and revitalization.

Competitive Bidding - Coordinated **competitive bidding** for all subcontracted electrical, HVAC and site work for the $20 million Haynes Industrial Project.

Construction Management - Directed **construction management** affairs for the renovation of the Inner Harbor Tunnel, a 5-year, $2.8 billion project.

Construction Trades - Supervised all **construction trades** and field crews of up to 400 at six major job sites throughout Dallas.

Contract Administration - Managed **contract administration** function for DOE-funded R&D facilities.

Contract Award - Reviewed competitive bids and managed **contract award** to best-price, best-quality supplier.

Critical Path Method (CPM) Scheduling - Introduced **CPM scheduling** and reduced manhours by 15%.

Design & Engineering - Led **design and engineering** teams responsible for proposal development and final contract delivery.

Divestiture - Directed **divestiture** of $50 million in non-performing real estate assets.

Engineering Change Orders (ECOs) - Transmitted **ECOs** to all project personnel and coordinated follow-up with all trades.

Estimating - Managed **estimating** and produced specifications for over $1 billion in annual real estate development and renovation projects.

Environmental Compliance - Reviewed all project plans and specifications to ensure stringent **environmental compliance** with corporate policy and federal regulations.

Facilities Management - Senior Director responsible for **facilities management**, new construction and renovation of over $200 million in corporate real estate assets.

Fair Market Value Pricing - Established **fair market value pricing** for all asset sales and liquidations.

Field Construction Management - Full supervisory responsibility for **field construction management**, crewing and schedule control on fast-track restaurant projects.

Grounds Maintenance - Directed 200-person staff and controlled $55 million annual operating budget for the Smithsonian's **ground maintenance** operations.

Historic Property Renovation - Founded real estate investment firm specializing in **historic property renovation** and resale to public agencies and municipalities.

Industrial Development - Partnered with business leaders to fund **industrial development** projects in major metropolitan areas throughout the Southwestern U.S.

Infrastructure Development - Managed $10 million investment in **infrastructure development**, including all site work, paving and common areas.

Leasing Management - Designed and directed **leasing management** programs for large office complexes in Midtown Manhattan.

Master Community Association - Appointed as the Corporate Representative to the **Master Community Association**, working cooperatively with residents to develop bylaws, policies and operating procedures.

Master Scheduling - Implemented a **master scheduling** program which measurably expedited schedule completion and compliance.

Mixed Use Property - Funded development of over $25 million in **mixed use property** as part of Baltimore's Inner Harbor revitalization.

Occupancy - Designed tenant incentive programs to optimize **occupancy** and retention.

Planned Use Development (PUD) - Member of Jim Rouse's senior management team leading the development of one of the first **PUD** projects in the U.S. (Columbia, Maryland).

Portfolio - Challenged to strengthen the financial and competitive value of property **portfolio**, increase ROI and improve investor credibility.

Preventive Maintenance - Designed a scheduled **preventive maintenance** program, virtually eliminating all major building and systems problems (calculated at a better than $250,000 annual cost savings).

Project Concept - Drove **project concept** for the first-ever downtown entertainment center in Morristown integrating creative arts, theatrical production and recreational programming.

Project Development - Guided **project development** as the direct liaison between developer, investors, bankers and community leaders.

Project Management - Senior Executive with full responsibility for all bidding, proposals, contract awards and **project management** for Mattel's new facility construction projects.

Project Scheduling - Streamlined and expedited **project scheduling**, reporting and documentation requirements.

Property Management - Directed leasing, tenant relations and **property management** for a 202-tenant apartment complex with full amenities and service programs.

Property Valuation - Guided **property valuation** for all proposed land and commercial property acquisitions.

Real Estate Appraisal - Managed **real estate appraisal** for leased and sold properties.

Real Estate Brokerage - Launched new venture and built one of the most successful and most profitable **real estate brokerages** in Miami, Florida.

Real Estate Development - Formed limited partnerships to fund over $500 million in healthcare **real estate development** projects in revitalized inner cities.

Real Estate Investment Trust (REIT) - Managed a $2.6 billion **REIT** for the Triple XXX Investment Group, improving investment returns by an average of 10%-12% annually.

Real Estate Law - Combined general management and **real estate law** expertise to return Andersen Properties to profitability.

Real Estate Partnership - Structured and negotiated **real estate partnership** with 3M to build R&D and manufacturing facilities throughout the Far East.

Regulatory Compliance - Achieved/surpassed all **regulatory compliance** objectives for 10 consecutive years.

Renovation - Directed 60-person crew on $500,000 million **renovation** and expansion of corporate training center.

Return on Assets (ROA) - Improved **ROA** by 16% on all divested properties through more aggressive negotiations.

Return on Equity (ROE) - Acquired, renovated and divested six commercial properties for a 26% **ROE**.

Return on Investment (ROI) - Negotiated acquisition of six industrial plants in Southwestern Mississippi, partnered with local manufacturers and delivered a 49% **ROI** to principals.

Site Development - Managed preliminary $2 million **site development** project for a proposed 500-home residential subdivision.

Site Remediation - Directed **site remediation** projects to eliminate hazardous conditions and pollutants.

Specifications - Authored project **specifications** for the $2.8 million renovation of the Walker-Schmidt Fidelity Building in downtown Minneapolis.

Syndications - Structured, negotiated and formed several real estate **syndications** in cooperation with private investor groups nationwide.

Tenant Relations - Significantly improved **tenant relations** through introduction of monthly tenant newsletter and monthly tenant meetings.

Tenant Retention - Renovated facility and improved **tenant retention** by 20% over previous year.

Turnkey Construction - Managed over $300 million in **turnkey construction** projects for client companies nationwide.

LOUISE A. ROBINSON, RPA

92 Adelaide Street
Belleville, Missouri 60133

Phone (601) 538-3229
Fax (601) 538-3532

REAL ESTATE INDUSTRY PROFESSIONAL
Property Management / Marketing / Tenant Relations

Twenty years experience in commercial and residential real estate. Consistently successful in increasing revenues, occupancy and income through expertise in building tenant relations and responding to tenant needs. Extensive qualifications in property/site renovation and construction, multi-year competitive leasing, multi-site property management and cost control/reduction. Outstanding communication and interpersonal relations skills.

PROFESSIONAL EXPERIENCE:

Property Manager   1992 to Present
A-ONE PROPERTIES, INC., Clifton, Missouri

Portfolio: *163,000 square feet of prime office space in a 3-building complex on 9 acres with large parking lots and extensive landscaping. Asset value of $13.5 million.*

Recruited as the Property Manager with full P&L responsibility for the entire portfolio. Scope of responsibility includes construction, renovation, tenant relations/retention, collections, outsourcing, contract negotiations, purchasing, monthly financial reporting and general office/administrative affairs.

- Increased occupancy from 29% to 73% in less than three years through personal efforts in property improvement and extensive networking leasing efforts with realtors and brokers.
- Led the strategic planning and preparation of fiscal and calendar budgets. Maintained financial control of forecasted budget. Brought 1996 under budget.
- Managed, in conjunction with project manager, $1.5 million renovation of all common areas. Delivered project on-time and within budget.
- Negotiated outsourcing contracts for facilities maintenance/repair, janitorial services and property security. Consistently reduced expenses while increasing quality of service and tenant satisfaction.

Vice President / Property Manager   1991 to 1992
THE REAL PROPERTY CORPORATION, Lewis, Missouri

Portfolio: *230,000 square feet comprised of 3 office buildings and 11 luxury garden apartment complexes. Asset value of $36 million.*

Led the successful turnaround of the portfolio to meet investor and owner financial objectives. Held full responsibility for marketing, construction and renovation, tenant relations, cash flow management, financial reporting and general administrative affairs. Spearheaded a high-profile marketing and public relations initiative to upgrade tenant quality. Directed a staff of 30.

- Worked with architects and contractors in the space planning and tenant fit-up of all leased space.
- Managed a large-scale renovation to upgrade the facilities, properties and common areas of the portfolio as part of the initiative to increase tenant retention and improve market competitiveness.
- Negotiated/directed all maintenance and improvement work including electrical systems, HVAC, elevators and grounds. Designed a preventive maintenance program to reduce expenditures.

Chief Operating Officer   1990 to 1991
GRIFFITH MANAGEMENT CORPORATION, Wayne, Missouri

Portfolio: Mid-sized commercial office building. Asset value of $4.5 million.

Recruited for one-year special project to direct a complete facilities renovation to transition property into the 1990's. Directed a number of site improvement projects, expanded and upgraded existing spaces, and designed tenant/owner communication programs.

• Worked with leading brokers to increase occupancy by 30%-35% through extension of existing tenant leases and negotiation of new, long-term tenant leases. Increased property value by 28% in one year.

Association Manager   1988 to 1990
HILLS VILLAGE ASSOCIATION, Bedminster, Missouri

Portfolio: 153-acre, 1492-unit Association with 4000+ residents.

Challenged to manage a master community association for one of the largest planned urban developments (PUD) in the U.S. Established policies and procedures, developed organizational infrastructure and created cooperative working relationships between home owners, builders and investors.

President / Broker / Managing Partner / Property Manager   1979 to 1988
THE ROBINSON MANAGEMENT GROUP, INC., Montclair, Missouri

As President of The Robinson Group, represented sellers, buyers and investors in commercial real estate sales transactions totalling several million dollars. As President of Bamberger Management Company, held full P&L responsibility for the management of 2500 residential and commercial units at 12 properties throughout the region.

EDUCATION & PROFESSIONAL CERTIFICATIONS: ▬▬▬▬▬▬▬▬▬

Certified Property Manager (CPM) Candidate, Institute of Real Estate Management, Current
Real Property Administrator (RPA), Building Owners and Managers Association, 1993
Registered Property Manager (RPM), International Real Estate Institute, 1993
New Jersey Licensed Real Estate Broker, Since 1975

PROFESSIONAL AFFILIATIONS: ▬▬▬▬▬▬▬▬▬

National Association of Corporate Real Estate Executives (NACORE)
Building Owners and Managers Association International (BOMA)
Institute of Real Estate Management (IREM)
Industrial and Commercial Real Estate Women (ICREW)
International Real Estate Institute (IREI)

RETAIL

Positions

Assistant Store Manager
Associate Store Manager
Buyer
Department Manager
Director of Retail Operations
Director of Retail Sales
District Manager
District Vice President
General Manager
Manager in Training
Merchandise Manager
Personnel Scheduling Coordinator
Regional Manager
Retail Sales Associate
Retail Sales Manager
Senior Buyer
Senior Merchandiser
Senior Sales Associate
Store Manager
Store Operations Manager
Vice President of Retail Operations
Vice President of Retail Sales

KeyWords

Buyer Awareness - Conceived and directed production of new creative campaign to increase **buyer awareness** and solidify market positioning.

Credit Operations - Restructured **credit operations**, implemented more stringent credit authorization procedures, and reduced bad debt by 12% in FY96.

Customer Loyalty - Created Neiman's first-ever **customer loyalty** programs, positioning the organization as a pioneer in innovative customer service and delivery.

Customer Service - Revitalized the organization's commitment to **customer service**, introduced a series of customer premiums and incentive programs, and dominated retail market.

District Sales - Recruited to turnaround **district sales** operations encompassing 54 retail stores, 500+ employees and over $260 million in annual sales.

Distribution Management - Structured a multi-site **distribution management** and inventory control program to reduce product losses, cut staffing costs and decrease transportation time.

Hardgoods - Directed a $500 million retail **hardgoods** sales operation that achieved/surpassed annual revenue and profit goals by an average of 12%-15%.

In-Store Promotions - Led creative team responsible for design, production and placement of **in-store promotions**, POS displays and credit card incentive campaigns.

Inventory Control - Restructured documentation and reporting requirements for all incoming merchandise to improve **inventory control** and management competencies.

Inventory Shrinkage - Implemented internal control procedures and reduced **inventory shrinkage** by more than 8% annually (despite consistent and significant employee turnover).

Loss Prevention - Designed **loss prevention programs** that reduced customer theft by more than 20% and employee theft by 10%.

Mass Merchants - Negotiated $200 million in exclusive product sales with **mass merchants** nationwide (e.g., WalMart, Rose's, Hill's).

Merchandising - Revitalized Macy's **merchandising** operations, recruited five experienced retail merchandisers and contributed to a solid 10% increase in 1996 sales revenues.

Multi-Site Operations - Senior Business Executive responsible for **multi-site operations** throughout the Midwestern U.S, including 200 company stores, 150 franchise stores and more than 3000 employees.

POS Promotions - Designed award-winning POS **promotions** honored for excellence in "creative concept" and "tactical execution" at the industry's 1996 annual conference.

Preferred Customer Management - Created a **preferred customer management** program in cooperation with Sales, Merchandising and Purchasing that drove sales growth within niche markets by more than 35%.

Pricing - Restructured product **pricing** and improved bottom-line profits throughout all departments by a minimum of 5%.

Product Management - Segmented product lines and introduced a new **product management** function focused on customer demand and product movement.

Retail Sales - Senior Operating Executive with full responsibility for the strategic planning, staffing, budgeting, MIS, warehousing, distribution, facilities, sales and service operations of a $2.8 billion specialty **retail sales** chain.

Security Operations - Revitalized in-store **security operations**, retrained staff and reduced in-store theft by 24%.

Softgoods - Recruited to rebuild Maxwell's **softgoods** operations to compete with leading specialty retailers and accelerate market gains.

Specialty Retailer - Raised $25 million in private financing to fund the acquisition and expansion of a 4-store **specialty retailer** poised for strong market growth.

Stock Management - Introduced stringent **stock management** and documentation procedures to better control over $400 million in incoming merchandise annually.

Warehousing Operations - Restructured **warehousing operations** from company-owned to commercially-leased facilities and reduced annual product storage costs by more than 18%.

CHARLES P. WILSON
1428 Ocean View Drive
New Orleans, Louisiana 33626
(514) 675-8723

MANAGEMENT PROFILE
Multi-Site Retail & Service Operations / Franchise & Company-Owned Operations

Dynamic management career with start-up, turnaround and high-growth organizations. Cross-functional expertise in business planning, marketing, operations management, human resources and finance. Delivered strong revenue and profit results within highly competitive markets. PC proficient.

Characterized as a strong and decisive business leader. Excellent problem solving, communication, interpersonal relations and "call to action" skills.

PROFESSIONAL EXPERIENCE:

KWIK LUBE INTERNATIONAL, INC.   1993 to Present

Regional Manager / District Manager

Returned to Kwik Lube after nine years of general management and P&L management positions with two large Louisiana-based franchisees. Hold direct P&L responsibility for up to 37 sales/service centers throughout Louisiana. Led a team of four District Managers.

Scope of responsibility is includes marketing and new business development, management training and development, sales/service training, budgeting, accounting, auditing and financial reporting. Challenged to introduce improved business and operating processes to drive revenue growth, reduce operating costs and improve net profitability of multi-site operations.

- Delivered strong and sustainable financial results:
  − Met/exceeded all profit budgets each consecutive year.
  − Delivered 2.3% sales increase and 12.6% profit improvement in $14 million organization.
  − Delivered 4.2% sales increase and 13.3% profit improvement in $7 million organization.
- Ranked as the #1 region in the U.S. for customer satisfaction ratings.
- Currently spearheading start-up of new strategic partnership with Sears (nationwide program). Leading the development of three pilot operations in Louisiana to evaluate operational feasibility of new partnership. To date, delivered $500,000 in first year sales revenues.

SMITH PETROLEUM COMPANY (Kwik Lube Franchise)   1988 to 1993

General Manager

Promoted from District Manager to General Manager with full P&L responsibility for the management of 11 operating locations throughout the South Coast of Louisiana. Led a team of two District Managers directing daily sales and service operations.

Focused efforts on building revenues and profitability. Redesigned and strengthened advertising/marketing programs, streamlined administrative processes, improved budget and financial controls, and upgraded recruitment and training programs. Launched internal reorganization and operations redesign initiative.

CHARLES P. WILSON - *Page Two*

SMITH PETROLEUM COMPANY *(Continued)*

- Built annual sales revenues from $3 million to $4.2 million, transitioned the operation from loss to breakeven and took negative cash flow to positive within one year.
- Facilitated implementation of POS technology with PC network to enhance internal sales controls and reporting capabilities.
- Designed incentive program and reduced operating costs by $500,000.
- Hired local advertising agency and directed multimedia print, broadcast and direct mail campaigns.
- Led new store openings, divestitures and aggressive turnaround initiatives.

GULF AUTOMOTIVE SERVICES (Kwik Lube Franchise)   1984 to 1987

Director of Operations

Recruited by owner to lead the franchisee through a period of rapid growth and expansion. Challenged to build organizational infrastructure, strengthen operations, recruit/train personnel and spearhead aggressive marketing/business development initiatives. Held full P&L responsibility. Led a team of two District Managers.

- Led the organization through a period of accelerated growth and expansion, from 6 to 12 locations and from 36 to 100+ employees. Built annual sales from $1.5 million to $3.5 million.
- Facilitated profitable integration of three Pennzoil operations into existing franchise.

NOTE: In July 1987, Kwik Lube bought back the franchise. Remained as Director of Operations through March 1988 when acquired by Smith Petroleum Company.

KWIK LUBE INTERNATIONAL, INC.   1981 to 1984

Operations Consultant / Training Director (1983 to 1984)
Operations Assistant (1982 to 1983)
Unit Manager (1982)
Manager Trainee (1981 to 1982)

Fast-track promotion through early professional career. Highlights included:

- Consulted with franchise owners in the Baltimore, Philadelphia and South New Jersey markets to provide expertise in operations, auditing, compliance and new store openings.
- Led basic and advanced operations training courses to store managers and franchise owners to enhance their competencies in operations, product knowledge, inventory control, scheduling, expense control and staffing/manpower planning.
- Managed new unit from pre-opening, staffing, initial marketing/business development, start-up and grand opening through transition to independent franchisee.

EDUCATION: **BS Degree**, Bridgewater College, Bridgewater, Virginia, 1981
The Dale Carnegie Course, 1984
The Centers for Values Research Training, 1985

SALES & MARKETING

NOTE: *Although the two functions are uniquely distinct, Sales & Marketing were integrated into one section due to the significant overlap in position titles, functions, responsibilities and achievements.*

Positions

Account Executive

Account Manager

Account Representative

Brand Manager

Business Development Representative

Chief Marketing Officer

Customer Representative

Customer Sales Associate

Director of Business Development

Director of Marketing

Director of Marketing Communications

Director of Marketing Support

Director of Sales & Marketing

Director of Sales Support

District Manager

Division Sales Manager

Global Marketing Associate

Global Sales Executive

Global Sales Manager

International Sales Manager

Key Account Executive

Key Account Manager

Major Account Representative

Major Account Manager

Manufacturers' Representative

Market Research Associate

Marketing Analyst

Marketing Associate

Marketing Director

Marketing Manager

Marketing Representative

National Account Executive

National Account Manager

National Sales Manager

Product Manager

Product Line Manager

Regional Sales Manager

Sales Associate

Sales Director

Sales Manager

Sales Representative

Sales Trainer

Sales Training Manager

Senior Account Executive

Senior Sales Associate

Senior Vice President

Technical Marketing Associate

Technical Sales Representative

Territory Sales Manager

Territory Sales Representative

Vice President of Business Development

Vice President of Sales & Marketing

KeyWords

Account Development - Spearheaded **account development** programs throughout emerging markets worldwide.

Account Management - Profitably directed **account management** programs for key customers nationwide including Pepsi, Rolex and Time Warner.

Account Retention - Created innovative **account retention** programs to protect key customer against competition.

Brand Management - Instituted a formal **brand management** process to accelerate revenue growth within the company's core product line.

Business Development - Launched new **business development** initiatives throughout emerging Latin American markets.

Campaign Management - Directed copywriting, graphics and multimedia production personnel to create an integrated **campaign management** strategy.

Competitive Analysis - Managed 6-person cross-functional marketing team responsible for **competitive analysis** and trend modeling within the mature hardlines market.

Competitive Contract Award - Favorably positioned negotiations to win **competitive contract award** against three major automotive manufacturers.

Competitive Market Intelligence - Compiled historical data, forecasts and projections for a comprehensive **competitive market intelligence** study.

Competitive Product Positioning - Realigned sales and distribution channels to enhance **competitive product positioning** and accelerate revenue performance.

Consultative Sales - Deployed IBM's first-ever **consultative sales** and account management programs focusing on customer needs assessment, technology delivery and long-term customer training/support.

Customer Loyalty - Initiated pioneering programs in **customer loyalty** to halt competition.

Customer Needs Assessment - Led organization-wide analyses to develop a comprehensive **customer needs assessment** and retention program.

Customer Retention - Improved **customer retention** ratings by 26% through the introduction of sales incentives, premiums and targeted promotions.

Customer Satisfaction - Increased **customer satisfaction** ratings with the implementation of account management and retention strategies.

Customer Service - Managed a fully-integrated **customer service** function comprised of personnel from Sales, Marketing, Order Fulfillment, Distribution and Customer Training/Support.

Direct Mail Marketing - Orchestrated copywriting, design and print production of a 20,000-piece **direct mail marketing campaign** to support new product launch.

Direct Response Marketing - Deployed multimedia advertising and promotions to create a high-impact **direct response campaign** with better than 72% customer response.

Direct Sales - Managed a 65-person **direct sales** organization throughout North America.

Distributor Management - Recruited, trained and directed worldwide **distributor management** programs to augment direct sales team.

Emerging Markets - Researched global sales trends and identified the top performing **emerging markets** worldwide as the first step in new product placement and positioning.

Field Sales Management - Promoted to **field sales management** position responsible for 22 direct sales associates and a 65-person North American distribution network.

Fulfillment - Reengineered core business processes to enhance the order **fulfillment** and distribution process.

Global Markets - Introduced new product technology to launch Zenith into key **global markets**.

Global Sales - Built and managed American Airlines' most profitable **global sales** organization.

Headquarters Account Management - Assigned full P&L responsibility for **headquarters account management** of the Marriott business relationship.

High-Impact Presentations - Created multimedia, **high-impact presentations** to win a $5 million, 5-year customer contract.

Incentive Planning - Devised unique **incentive planning** program that drove individual sales performance by better than 10% in 1996.

Indirect Sales - Created **indirect sales** channels throughout the Mid-Atlantic integrating the talents and resources of VARs, resellers and other third-party distributors.

International Sales - Exploded **international sales** revenues with launch throughout Eastern Europe.

International Trade - Led AMAX's **international trade**, barter and import/export programs.

Key Account Management - Innovated a unique **key account management** program targeted to the company's 10 largest multinational clients within North America.

Line Extension - Facilitated core product **line extension** in response to changing consumer market demands.

Margin Improvement - Streamlined field sales programs and consolidated functions, resulting in a 16% **margin improvement** on all major product lines.

Market Launch - Directed **market launch** of six new products in 1996, delivering total revenues of more than $2.8 million (125% of quota).

Market Positioning - Evaluated competitive activity and defined new corporate strategy for **market positioning** and revenue growth.

Market Research - Formalized Hill Brothers' **market research** function with the introduction of real-time data access to competitive trends, products, technologies and markets.

Market Share Ratings - Created a unique customer premium program and improved **market share ratings** by 16% in FY96.

Market Surveys - Developed a portfolio of **market surveys**, customer questionnaires and consumer buying observational tools to define long-term product positioning.

Marketing Strategy - Conceived the **marketing strategy** that drove Procter & Gamble to its most profitable year within the consumer goods and HBA industries.

Mass Merchants - Challenged to identify and capitalize upon sales opportunities within emerging **mass merchants** market.

Multi-Channel Distribution - Expanded sales penetration through development of **multi-channel distribution** programs in Latin America, South Africa and the Pacific Rim.

Multi-Channel Sales - Led a **multi-channel sales** organization integrating direct, distributor and VAR sales teams.

Multimedia Advertising - Launched Discovery's **multimedia advertising** program (e.g., print, broadcast, cable, Internet) in cooperation with one of New York's most prestigious advertising agencies.

Multimedia Marketing Communications - Integrated print, broadcast, cable and Internet technologies to create high-impact, high-yield, **multimedia marketing communications** targeted to customers nationwide.

National Account Management - Integrated the resources, products and technologies of all of Microsoft's customer sales divisions to create a fully-integrated **national account management** organization.

Negotiations - Led high-powered **negotiations** for the successful award of a $6.2 million federal contract.

New Market Development - Hand-selected by CEO to spearhead Marriott's **new market development** program as the first step in a 10-year global expansion plan.

New Product Introduction - Led the development and market launch of all new **product introduction** programs for Mazda, exceeding revenue goals by 22% and strengthening the company's long-term market position.

Product Development - Spearheaded new **product development** programs, from concept through design, prototyping and testing, to final market launch.

Product Launch - Led six new **product launch** campaigns within the emerging Eastern European markets, with one product generating $2.6 million in first year revenues (167% of quota).

Product Lifecycle Management - Directed "cradle-to-grave" **product lifecycle management** programs in cooperation with Engineering, Marketing, Sales and Distribution.

Product Line Rationalization - Revitalized Sperry's **product line rationalization** program, divested two non-performing lines and redeployed assets to focus on long-term growth markets.

Product Positioning - Evaluated competitive market trends and implemented **product positioning** strategies to ensure long-term and sustainable growth.

Profit & Loss (P&L) Management - Held full **P&L management** responsibility for the company's core product line and all line extensions.

Promotions - Conceived, developed and launched multimedia **promotions** that dominated the regional market.

Profit Growth - Reengineered field sales and distribution organizations despite corporate downsizing and delivered a 16% gain in **profit growth** (versus 5% industry-wide loss).

Public Relations - Created Martin Marietta's corporate **public relations** function and produced an average of 10 press releases per month for the *Wall Street Journal* and *New York Times*.

Public Speaking - Traveled worldwide to lead **public speaking** engagements on behalf of the corporation during its transition from private to public ownership.

Revenue Growth - Exploded market penetration and drove a 46% gain in **revenue growth** within first six months.

Revenue Stream - Created new **revenue stream** with the introduction of products throughout the Far Eastern market.

Sales Closing - Dominated sales negotiations and favorably positioned **sales closing** against competition.

Sales Cycle Management - Spearheaded the entire **sales cycle management** process, from initial client consultation and needs assessment through product demonstration, price and service negotiations, and final sales closings.

Sales Forecasting - Introduced real-time data exchange between global sales offices to expedite annual **sales forecasting** functions.

Sales Training - Created a 6-month intensive **sales training** program in basic selling skills, competitive negotiations and customer development/retention.

Sales Presentations - Devised winning **sales presentations** utilizing multimedia demonstration techniques to consistently outperformed competition.

Solutions Selling - Delivered **solutions selling** strategies to enhance revenue performance of field sales organization.

Strategic Market Planning - Facilitated annual **strategic market planning** sessions in cooperation with top-level executives, sales and marketing managers, product line managers, manufacturing director and other key management staff.

Tactical Market Plans - Translated marketing strategy into **tactical market plans** to accelerate growth throughout North America.

Team Building/Leadership - Spearheaded first-ever **team building/leadership** programs as the platform for merging the competencies of several distinct product lines and business units.

Trend Analysis - Devised innovative research and statistical methods to strengthen **trend analysis**, market analysis and competitive analysis competencies.

MARGARET E. APPLEGATE
3984 Soldier Trail
Bellevue, Washington 98332

Phone (206) 488-8724   Fax (206) 488-7762

SENIOR SALES & MARKETING EXECUTIVE
Domestic & International Business Development

*Strategic Marketing Planning / Competitive Market Positioning / Multi-Channel Distribution
Sales Training & Team Leadership / New Product Launch / New Market Development*

Dynamic sales and marketing management career delivering state-of-the-art technology worldwide. Achieved strong and sustainable revenue, market and profit contributions through expertise in business development, organizational development and performance management. Keen presentation, negotiation, communication and cross-cultural skills. Fluent in French (speaking, reading, writing). Understanding of Spanish and Italian. Member of American Management Association, International Trade Association and Women in Technology.

PROFESSIONAL EXPERIENCE

Vice President - Americas Operations
International Software, Inc., Seattle, Washington (1995 to Present)

Recruited to $750 million NYSE company (one of the world's largest software providers with customer base including the top Fortune 500 corporations). Challenged to plan and orchestrate an aggressive turnaround and rejuvenation of the Americas sales organization.

Scope of responsibility includes all sales, marketing, business development, channel development and customer management/retention operations throughout South America, Central America, Mexico and the Caribbean. Lead a team of 12 regional managers, product specialists and administrative personnel. Manage a 30-person direct sales force in Brazil.

- Transitioned Americas organization from 44% of plan in 1995 to 112% of plan in 1996 ($7 million to $14+ million).

- Expanded distributor base by more than 50% to increase market penetration and facilitate market launch of new product technologies and services.

- Provided strong organizational leadership and active participation in key account sales and business development. Resulted in a significant gain in employee morale, productivity and sales production.

- Concurrent P&L responsibility for independent Brazilian-based sales and marketing company. Delivered 45% growth within less than one year through development of multinational customer base. Currently facilitating market introduction of EDI sales group with first year revenue projections at $1+ million.

Managing Partner
TechCom, Inc., Washington, D.C. (1994 to 1995)

Founded international software distribution company focusing on distributed and systems software productivity tools (emphasis on DB2, Oracle and Sybase operating systems). Created marketing strategies, communications, promotional materials, reseller channels and in-house sales programs. Developed partnering program for export/import of software services.

Director & General Manager - International Sales Operations
Global Systems Corporation, Washington, D.C. (1986 to 1994)

Fast-track promotion through four increasingly responsible international management assignments to final position as Senior Executive directing worldwide software sales and marketing operations for direct and reseller channels. Managed UK-based European operation and a team of sales, marketing and technical support managers.

- Increased Global's international sales operation from a $3 million, six-country region to a $30 million, 50-country worldwide sales organization representing 53% of corporate revenue.

- Established international reseller network to market distributed computing solutions for UNIX platforms including IBM AIX, HP-UX, Sun OS and Sun Solaris.

- Expanded and restructured sales networks in Western Europe, Eastern Europe, South America and the Pac Rim through development of distributor channels for Global's Performance Series for MVS and VSE.

- Renegotiated software agreement with European distributors, saving $5 million in contract dissolution compensation. Successfully renegotiated distribution agreements during product divestiture, resulting in a $9 million savings to Global.

- Reviewed and approved multinational software sales contracts with Fortune 100 companies.

- Honored for outstanding sales results and over-quota production for eight consecutive years.

Manager of Field Marketing - North American Sales Operations
Data Management, Inc., Alexandria, Virginia / Seattle, Washington (1979 to 1986)
(Acquired by International Software)

Marketing Executive with full responsibility for the design, development and implementation of marketing programs for 15 U.S. offices and Canada on behalf of one of the world's largest independent software vendors. Liaison between North American Operations and International Division.

- Created innovative incentive programs and facilitated training programs for field sales and marketing teams. Coordinated week-long, annual worldwide sales and technical conference.

- Designed marketing collateral and promotional materials for use by North American sales offices.

- Expanded North American sales/marketing presence through participation in industry trade shows, conventions and exhibits targeted to both commercial and Federal sectors.

- Initiated nationwide seminar program to promote DMI's software products. Designed seminar materials, directed presentation programs and spearheaded implementation of computer-based lead tracking system.

Previous Professional Positions

Assistant to the Corporate Vice President of Public Relations, XT-Systems, Inc.
Executive Assistant - International Department, Trammel Crow Company

EDUCATION

B.A., San Francisco College of Women
Graduate Study/Psychology, University of Geneva - Switzerland

SECURITY & LAW ENFORCEMENT

Positions

Corporate Security Manager

Detective

Director of Corporate Security

Director of Industrial Security

Industrial Security Manager

Police Officer

Risk Management Specialist

Safety Officer

Security Manager

Security Officer

Supervisor of Detectives

Vice President of Corporate Security

Vice President of Industrial Security

KeyWords

Asset Protection - Directed **asset protection** programs for U.S. embassies and consulates worldwide (total asset value in excess of $20 billion).

Community Outreach - Managed **community outreach** and community policing programs throughout the Detroit metro region as part of the Department's long-term commitment to cooperative community relations.

Corporate Fraud - Managed sensitive investigations of **corporate fraud** totalling in the millions of dollars and perpetrated over the past five years.

Corporate Security - Member of 6-person Senior Management Team and the most Senior **Corporate Security** Executive responsible for facilities, VIP protection and intelligence.

Crisis Communications - Coordinated press relations and media interviews to expand **crisis communications** and outreach during LA riots.

Crisis Response - Manned and directed a 12-person **crisis response** team successful in resolving high-profile hostage situations.

Electronic Surveillance - Introduced **electronic surveillance** technology to improve physical security operations.

Emergency Planning & Response - Led the Department's annual **emergency planning and response** program in cooperation with local, state and federal law enforcement agencies throughout California.

Emergency Preparedness - Developed monthly **emergency preparedness** training and field exercises.

Industrial Espionage - Directed covert **industrial espionage** intelligence gathering and reporting to high-ranking military officials.

Industrial Security - Created **industrial security** programs to protect company facilities, technologies, products and other assets.

Interrogation - Directed **interrogation** in high-profile corporate fraud and espionage incidents.

Investigations Management - Coordinated worldwide **investigations management** team tracking the state's most wanted fugitives.

Law Enforcement - Advanced rapidly throughout 22-year **law enforcement** career, from initial field patrol through several investigative positions to final promotion to Chief of Police.

Media Relations - Appointed Departmental Spokesperson responsible for **media relations** and response to crisis situations.

Personal Protection - Provided **personal protection** services to top-ranking government, military and industry officials.

Public Relations - Promoted positive community relations through a proactive **public relations** initiative.

Safety Training - Designed in-house **safety training** programs for all personnel within Digital Equipment Corporation.

Security Operations - Integrated in-house and contract personnel to create full-scale corporate **security operations** at all BanCorp facilities.

Surveillance - Conducted field **surveillance** and documentation for organized crime investigations.

Tactical Field Operations - Promoted to Police Lieutenant responsible for **tactical field operations** and deployment in both routine and emergency situations.

VIP Protection - Charged with planning, staffing and all advance work for **VIP protection** programs worldwide.

White Collar Crime - Investigated alleged incidents of **white collar crime** throughout the emerging Internet and new media industries.

CHARLES E. FRANKLIN
1984 South Lincoln Avenue
Paramus, New Jersey 07665
(201) 654-9871

CAREER PROFILE:

LAW ENFORCEMENT OFFICER with 20+ years experience planning and managing Investigations, VIP Escort & Protection Service, Corporate & Industrial Site Security, Organized Crime and Intelligence. Strong qualification in budgeting, personnel affairs, training, resource management and emergency response. Excellent decision making and crisis management skills.

PROFESSIONAL EXPERIENCE:

MERCER CITY POLICE DEPARTMENT, Mercer, New Jersey   1975 to Present

Senior Staff Officer, Professional Standards Division (1994 to Present)
Commander, Special Investigations Unit (1990 to 1994)
Assistant Commander, Special Investigations Unit (1988 to 1990)
Sergeant, Detective Bureau (1985 to 1988)
Investigator/Detective (1980 to 1985)
Patrol Officer (1975 to 1980)

Promoted rapidly throughout law enforcement career, from early patrol assignments to most recent position directing high-profile special investigations. Supervised up to seven police officers and investigators. Directed case planning and management, personnel assignment, emergency preparedness and response, suspect interrogation, witness interviewing and all reporting/documentation. Special assignments and position highlights have included:

Special Investigations

- As Commander of the Special Investigations Unit, responsible for discreet investigations and intelligence gathering activities concerning organized gangs, criminal activities within law enforcement agencies, VIP security operations for local and foreign dignitaries, bias crime investigations (e.g., ethnic, race, religion, sexual orientation), drug trafficking, extortion, counterfeiting and other criminal activity.

- Deputized U.S. Marshall assigned to supervise Federal DEA wire tap room during a sensitive investigation of alleged police officer participation in cocaine distribution.

- Managed investigative operations in the Violent Crimes Unit, Burglary Squad, Street Crimes Unit and Robbery Squad.

VIP/Executive Security Operation

- Assigned to the Security Detail for the President of Greece. Worked in cooperation with the U.S. Secret Service and State Department to coordinate advance security, assess potential threats and provide security escort services throughout the area.

- Assisted in directing protection and security operations for the Pope during his visits throughout New York and New Jersey. Coordinated site assessments, security advance work and on-site protection in cooperation with various local, state and federal agencies.

CHARLES E. FRANKLIN - *Page Two*

Industrial Security Operations

- Conducted extensive site threat assessment for the Fourth of July Sailing Event in New York City. Produced aerial photography to monitor site and planned emergency unit availability/response.

- Managed site surveillance, perimeter searches, investigations and security planning efforts for corporate and industrial facilities throughout the New York/New Jersey metro region.

Hostage Negotiations

- Member of the Mercer City Police Department's Hostage Negotiating Team since 1989.

Professional Standards Division Operations

- Currently serve on the Deputy Chief's Staff with direct responsibility for coordinating operations between various units within the Division (e.g., Internal Affairs, Planning & Research, Inspectional Services, Medical Bureau, Police Academy, Pistol Range). Manage budget development/administration, officer assignment, recordkeeping, training coordination and other critical functions to ensure cooperative internal operations.

EDUCATION & SPECIALIZED TRAINING *(partial listing)*:

- Emergency Management: Incident Command System Training, 1995
- Special Tactics & Security, 1995
- Corporate Executive Protection, Corporate & Economic Espionage, 1994
- Symposium on Terrorism, 1994
- Asian Organized Crime, 1993
- Hazardous Material Awareness, 1993
- Hostage Negotiations, 1990
- Advanced Criminal Investigation, 1980
- Graduate, New Jersey Police Academy, 1975

PROFESSIONAL PROFILE:

Honors & Awards: 50 Excellent Police Service Awards, 15 Commendations, Combined P.O.B.A. Valor Awards, Fraternal Order of Police Citation, Kiwanis Club Unit Citation, NAACP Certificate of Merit, Mayor's Certificate of Award for Civil Contribution

Public Speaking: Asian Organized Crime, Law Enforcement Intelligence, Executive Protection

Military: Corporal, Military Police, U.S. Army (1971 to 1975)

TEACHING & EDUCATIONAL ADMINISTRATION

Positions

Academic Advisor
Academic Dean
Adjunct Professor
Administrator
Admissions Counselor
Assistant Dean
Associate Dean
Associate Professor
Center Director
Chancellor
Dean
Director
Educator
Executive Director
Financial Aid Director
Guidance Counselor
Instructor
President
Professor
Program Manager
Senior Instructor
Senior Vice President
Teacher
Trainer
Vice President of Academic Services
Vice President of Educational Services

KeyWords

Academic Advisement - Established an **academic advisement** program for both degree and non-degree seeking students.

Accreditation - Led the university through a two-year successful **accreditation** process.

Admissions Management - Restructured the college's **admissions management** process to encourage enrollment by minority, handicapped and other special populations.

Alumni Relations - Volunteered to build Catonsville Community College's first-ever formal **alumni relations** and giving program.

Campus Life - Introduced expanding educational, social and recreational programs into the **Campus Life** Department to enhance students' experiences.

Capital Giving Campaign - Planned and directed the annual **capital giving campaign** which raised $2.8 million (25% over goal).

Career Counseling - Created expanded **career counseling** programs targeted to non-degree seeking and continuing education students interested in professional, paraprofessional and vocational opportunities.

Career Development - Negotiated cooperative education programs with local universities to introduce on-site **career development** and training programs.

Classroom Management - Demonstrated expertise in **classroom management**, student relations and learner retention.

Course Design - Led 12-person team in **course design** for Mathematics, Engineering and Science.

Conference Management - Directed annual planning, staffing, budgeting and logistics for an 11-part **conference management** series.

Curriculum Development - Expanded **curriculum development** functions across all major academic disciplines to enhance the quality of education.

Educational Administration - Appointed Program Director with full responsibility for budgeting, staffing, teacher training, **educational administration** and Board of Regents reporting.

Enrollment - Forged strategic alliances with all public school systems to identify qualified applicants and drove a 16% increase in 1996 student **enrollment**.

Extension Program - Negotiated partnership with the University of Michigan for an off-campus **extension program** for hourly manufacturing workers.

Field Instruction - Designed and led **field instruction** programs in the Biological and Chemical Sciences.

Grant Administration - Responsible for **grant administration** of $2.2 million in funds.

Higher Education - Promoted programs and activities to promote high school students' appreciation for **higher education** opportunities.

Holistic Learning - Integrated Math, Science, Language and the Arts to create a **holistic learning** and study center for senior adults.

Instructional Media - Acquired **instructional media** to develop alternative educational programs in foreign language instruction.

Instructional Programming - Led 6-person task force in **instructional programming** across all core academic disciplines.

Intercollegiate Athletics - Coached soccer team to #1 standing in the regional **intercollegiate athletics** division.

Leadership Training - Designed and instructed **leadership training** programs for newly-appointed supervisors and team leaders.

Lifelong Learning - Lobbied before the state legislature for funds to promote **lifelong learning** within the community.

Management Development - Created innovative course offerings to strengthen **management development** opportunities for adult students seeking career promotion.

Peer Counseling - Identified need for immediate intervention and created a **peer counseling** program to link top-performers with students in crisis.

Program Development - Championed innovative **program development** projects to gain a competitive lead over other area colleges and universities.

Public/Private Partnerships - Structured and negotiated **public/private partnerships** to fund alternative career and job skills training programs.

Public Speaking - Recognized for expertise in **public speaking** before regulatory, accrediting and licensing boards.

Recruitment - Innovated strategies to accelerate **recruitment** and increase enrollment across all major academic disciplines.

Residential Life - Created a **residential life** program that rewarded students for peer counseling, student advisement and tutorial assistance.

Scholastic Standards - Enhanced **scholastic standards**, enabling the college to compete with area universities.

Seminar Management - Directed staff responsible for **seminar management** at off-campus sites throughout the State of Michigan.

Student Retention - Increased **student retention** by 28% despite the addition of two new colleges within the local area.

Student Services - Expanded **student services** to include a monthly guest speakers program, biannual competitive sporting events and one-on-one peer counseling.

Student-Faculty Relations - Restored **student-faculty relations** following student unrest.

Textbook Review - Led committee responsible for **textbook review**, selection and acquisition.

Training & Development - Established Motorola's in-house **training and development** center for hourly, staff, professional, technical, supervisory and executive personnel.

MARY B. WASHINGTON
152 Red House Drive
Summerville, South Carolina 28998
(816) 358-1324

EDUCATION SERVICES & PROGRAM ADMINISTRATOR

Talented Administrator with eight years of cross-functional experience in:

- Strategic Planning & Leadership
- Educational Programming & Services
- Teacher Training & Education
- Committee Leadership & Team Building
- Budgeting & Expense Control
- Curriculum Design & Development
- Student Placement & Advisement
- Community & Special Events

Excellent planning, analytical and organizational skills. Effective project leader able to facilitate cooperation among administrators, faculty, students and the community. MBA Degree.

PROFESSIONAL EXPERIENCE:

Coordinator of Curriculum & Instruction /Lead Instructor - Accounting   1990 to Present
BUSINESS & TECHNICAL INSTITUTE, Charleston, South Carolina

Senior Administrative Manager with this state/federally funded training center with 500+ students. Scope of management responsibility is diverse and includes strategic planning, budgeting, curriculum development, instruction, advisory affairs, faculty/staff development, accreditation and operations management. Assist Vice President of Instruction in directing a staff of three administrative personnel with full management oversight for 30+ full-time professors and adjunct faculty.

Curriculum Innovation

- Developed certificate of completion program for specific courses to provide students with immediate employment credentials while completing long-term coursework.
- Evaluated current curriculum to expand course offerings and effectively prepare students for professional employment in business, professional and technical fields.
- Led program development, textbook selection, instruction and student evaluation for the Accounting Department, and all related courses and certification programs.

Staff Development & Instruction

- Managed the recruitment, selection and training of nine new faculty members.
- Led a series of workshops, seminars and continuing education programs for all faculty.
- Conducted periodic reviews of instructors to evaluate workload, teaching methods, student interaction and overall performance. Coordinated workload scheduling for all faculty.

Articulation & Community Affairs

- Appointed representative for the Institute to promote programs and services, including participation in Career Day activities at high schools throughout the region. Achieved measurable increases in enrollment and community awareness.
- Launched innovative articulation program with several area high schools in a joint effort to provide technical training at the high school level.

Accreditation & Regulatory Compliance

- Led workshops for instructors and orchestrated the research, documentation and presentation of materials for accreditation through the Council on Occupational Education.
- Implemented Institutional Effectiveness System (IES) into all core instructional programs to streamline planning, evaluation and budgeting processes.
- Reviewed curriculum and programs to ensure compliance with state mandates. Facilitated integration and communication of changes/enhancements into existing programs.

Administration & Operations Management

- Designed, developed and implemented improved business processes to streamline operations and reduce overhead costs.
- Assisted departments in the preparation and submission of annual operating budgets.
- Approved purchase requisitions for materials, equipment and personnel.

COLLEGE OF CHARLESTON, Charleston, South Carolina   1989

Instructor - Business

Established program guidelines and taught a broad range of accounting and general business courses. Played a key role in expanding enrollment through personal commitment to curriculum development and quality instruction.

EARLY CORPORATE EXPERIENCE:

Advanced through increasingly responsible accounting, loan processing and auditing positions. Gained extensive experience in general accounting, credit management, internal controls, regulatory compliance, executive presentations and staff management. Career progression:

Senior Credit Auditor	**BANK SOUTH CORPORATION**	1984 to 1988
Supervisory Loan Specialist	**SMALL BUSINESS ADMINISTRATION**	1982 to 1984

EDUCATION:

MBA (Finance), Georgia State University, 1984
BA (German), Wake Forest University, 1982

Continuing Professional Education:
Completed more than 90 hours of professional education and training on subjects including Youth Apprenticeship, Distance Learning, Workkeys in Action and Computer Technology. Participated in several state and local Tech Prep conferences.

PROFESSIONAL AFFILIATIONS:

Board of Directors (Past), Habitat for Humanity

TRANSPORTATION

Positions

Director of Dispatch Operations
Director of Distribution
Director of Logistics
Director of Operations
Director of Operations Support
Director of Transportation
Dispatch Manager
Distribution Manager
Export Manager
Fleet Manager
General Manager
Import Manager
Logistics Manager
Operations Manager
Operations Supervisor
Terminal Manager
Terminal Operations Manager
Traffic Manager
Transportation Manager
Vice President of Distribution
Vice President of Logistics
Vice President of Operations
Vice President of Transportation
Warehouse Manager

KeyWords

Agency Operations - Transitioned from company-owned to **agency operations** at all major ports throughout North America, reducing net operating expenses by more than $15 million annually.

Asset Management - Directed **asset management** and allocation of more than $60 million in equipment.

Cargo Handling - Designed improved **cargo handling** procedures, reducing workers' compensation costs by 22% annually.

Carrier Management - Outsourced all transportation functions and designed operations for new **carrier management** program.

Common Carrier - Contracted with **common carrier** for the movement of freight from manufacturing to warehousing centers nationwide.

Container Transportation - Designed **container transportation** programs to optimize space utilization and provide small shippers with economical rates for international freight forwarding.

Contract Transportation Services - Replaced in-house freight management system with **contract transportation services**, significantly increasing customer satisfaction and retention while reducing costs approximately 10%.

Customer Delivery Operations - Revitalized **customer delivery operations** with a focus on staff training in customer service and communication skills.

Dedicated Logistics Operations - Recruited to Ryder's **dedicated logistics operations** to integrate traffic, dispatch, warehousing, shipping and customer management operations.

Dispatch Operations - Consolidated **dispatch operations** for four centers into one facility, reduced staff 64% and improved on-time delivery to a consistent 99%.

Distribution Management - Planned and directed **distribution management** across multiple channels throughout North America and Western Europe.

Driver Leasing - Introduced **driver leasing**, driver training and equipment rental programs to expand market research and meet changing customer demands.

Equipment Control - Implemented **equipment control** processes and reduced damage costs by more than $2 million annually.

Export Operations - Senior Logistics Executive with full P&L, operating, staffing and budgeting responsibility for all **export operations** to the Far East.

Facilities Management - Revitalized **facilities management** programs, reduced costs, improved staff competencies and enhanced reliability of building management systems.

Fleet Management - Directed **fleet management** and fleet service for 2000 company-owned vehicles.

Freight Consolidation - Established new **freight consolidation** center at the Port of Baltimore.

Freight Forwarding - Managed a 200-person **freight forwarding** operation managing freight movement for W.R. Grace, AlliedSignal and Sears.

Import Operations - Assessed the profitability of existing **import operations**, eliminated non-profitable business lines and transitioned organization from loss to sustained profitability.

Inbound Transportation - Built an $8 million facility to manage **inbound transportation** and freight forwarding.

Intermodal Transportation Network - Established an **intermodal transportation network** integrating rail, sea, air and truck to service customers worldwide.

Line Management - Directed **line management** throughout the Far Eastern Maritime Service.

Load Analysis - Computerized **load analysis** and planning functions for all shipping operations.

Logistics Management - Senior Operating Executive with full P&L responsibility for a dedicated and fully-integrated **logistics management** organization with 22 sites nationwide.

Maritime Operations - Launched a start-up venture servicing **maritime operations** worldwide with on-site stevedoring at ports in 62 countries.

Outbound Transportation - Assembled all commodities into a centralized **outbound transportation** center to reduce domestic and international freight forwarding and traffic costs.

Over-The-Road Transportation - Transitioned from **over-the-road transportation** to rail transportation to expedite customer delivery.

Port Operations - Directed staffing, budgeting, planning, asset management and transportation planning for **port operations** in New York, Boston, Atlanta and Miami.

Regulatory Compliance - Achieved/surpassed all **regulatory compliance** standards for both OSHA and DOT.

Route Planning/Analysis - Automated **route planning/analysis** functions, improved costing and upgraded customer service.

Route Management - Reconfigured **route management** programs to optimize personnel and equipment resources.

Safety Management - Identified need and developed a six-part **safety management** and training program for all newly-hired personnel.

Safety Training - Revitalized **safety training** program and reduced on-site work accidents by 89%.

Terminal Operations - Restructured high-volume **terminal operations** at the Port of Wilmington, reducing costs 20% and improving customer satisfaction ratings by 88%.

Traffic Planning - Introduced GPS and other technologies to improve **traffic planning** and routing capabilities.

Traffic Management - Designed improved processes and systems to enhance **traffic management**, reduce reliance on paper documentation and achieve all budgeted operating goals.

Transportation Planning - Directed **transportation planning** for all Caterpillar dealers and distributors nationwide.

Transportation Management - Redesigned Xerox's **transportation management** programs and saved the corporation over $10 million in annual traffic, warehousing and distribution costs.

Warehouse Management - Directed **warehouse management** operations for six facilities in the Northwestern U.S. distributing products throughout 16 states.

Workflow Optimization - Created performance-driven systems designed for **workflow optimization**, staff training, quality improvement and cost reduction.

LARRY P. DAWSON
65421 North Post Road
Virginia Beach, VA 23541
(757) 654-8971

PROFESSIONAL QUALIFICATIONS: TRAFFIC / TRANSPORTATION MANAGEMENT

Distinguished professional career directing the transportation of air and surface freight, personal property, parcels and hazardous materials worldwide. Equally extensive experience in rates and tariffs, multimodal freight and commercial airline load requirements.

Strong planning, organizational, logistics, TQM, human resources, training/development, budgeting, facilities, technology management and fleet management qualifications. Effective leader, decision-maker and operations manager.

PROFESSIONAL EXPERIENCE:

TRAFFIC / TRANSPORTATION MANAGEMENT SPECIALIST   1987 to 1997

Fast-track promotion through several increasingly responsible positions in traffic/transportation management with the U.S. Navy. Rank at discharge — Lieutenant Commander. Career highlights included:

Superintendent - Air/Sea Delivery Service (1993 to 1997)

Senior Operations Manager with direct responsibility for the strategic planning, staffing, budgeting, logistics, equipment resources and daily operations of the air/sea delivery operation based in Japan. Scope of responsibility included the efficient transport of personnel, materials, equipment, supplies and commodities throughout the Pacific Rim. Directed a staff of 182 personnel and administered a $750,000 annual operating budget.

Established policies and procedures to support transportation operations, developed/implemented safety training and support programs, and directly managed facilities and facility upgrades. Determined current and long-range equipment and technology requirements to support transportation operations.

Achievements:

• Directed the design and completion of a $200,000 facility construction project which now serves as the model for U.S. Navy operations worldwide.

• Resolved long-standing staffing issues through redesign of critical support positions and brought staffing from 60% to 100% to meet operational requirements.

• Reduced cargo processing delays by 75% through design and implementation of improved handling, staffing and documentation procedures.

Superintendent - Air Freight Operations (1987 to 1992)

Promoted through a series of increasingly responsible air freight operations management positions in the U.S., Korea and Philippines. Served as Superintendent of Air Freight Operations, Air Terminal Manager, Passenger Services Manager and Aircraft Warehouse Manager. Personally directed over 65% of the nation's strategic air/sea operations and moved the largest volume of cargo in the Department of the Navy.

Held significant decision-making responsibility for personnel, equipment, logistics, facilities, budgets and operations planning/improvement. Trained/supervised up to 65 military and 30 civilian personnel. Controlled $8 million in fleet and technical resources for the movement of more than 45,000 tons of cargo and mail. Managed 66,000 square feet of warehousing, transportation and support facilities. Demonstrated superior planning and organization skills.

Achievements:

- Improved aircraft/fleet departure reliability rates by 100% (unprecedented in such a large and diverse operation).

- Led a series of facility improvement projects, several of which now serve as flagships for other transportation operations worldwide.

- Designed and directed implementation of computerized transportation operational support and training programs (e.g., planning, staffing, documentation, analysis). Led to measurable improvements in operational efficiency, reliability and quality while consistently reducing errors and time required for specific tasks.

- Planned and successfully managed massive freight operations initiated in response to crisis situations (e.g., Operations Desert Shield/Storm, Philippine earthquake).

EDUCATION:

B.A. in Transportation Management, 1987
OLD DOMINION UNIVERSITY, Richmond, Virginia

Highlights of Continuing Professional Education:

- Air/Sea Transportation Management
- Operational Support
- Officer Candidate School

CHAPTER 3

ACTION VERBS, HIGH-IMPACT PHRASES & PERSONALITY DESCRIPTORS

For Professionals, Managers & Senior Executives

Action Verbs

Use these Words to describe your responsibilities and highlight your achievements.

Accelerate	Assemble
Accomplish	Assess
Achieve	Assist
Acquire	Author
Adapt	Authorize
Address	Brief
Advance	Budget
Advise	Build
Advocate	Calculate
Analyze	Capture
Apply	Catalog
Appoint	Champion
Arbitrate	Chart
Architect	Clarify
Arrange	Classify
Ascertain	Close

Coach

Collect

Command

Communicate

Compare

Compel

Compile

Complete

Compute

Conceive

Conclude

Conduct

Conserve

Consolidate

Construct

Consult

Continue

Contract

Convert

Coordinate

Correct

Counsel

Craft

Create

Critique

Decrease

Define

Delegate

Deliver

Demonstrate

Deploy

Design

Detail

Detect

Determine

Develop

Devise

Direct

Discover

Dispense

Display

Distribute

Diversify

Divert

Document

Double

Draft

Drive

Earn

Edit

Educate

Effect

Elect

Eliminate

Emphasize

Enact

Encourage

Endure

Energize

Enforce

Engineer

Enhance

Enlist

Ensure

Establish

Estimate

Evaluate

Examine

Exceed

Execute

Exhibit

Expand

Expedite

Experiment

Export

Facilitate

Finalize

Finance

Forge

Form

Formalize

Formulate

Found

Generate

Govern

Graduate

Guide

Halt

Head

Hire

Honor

Hypothesize

Identify

Illustrate

Imagine

Implement

Import

Improve

Improvise

Increase

Influence

Inform

Initiate

Innovate

Inspect

Inspire

Install

Institute

Instruct

Integrate

Intensify

Interpret

Interview

Introduce

Invent

Inventory

Offer

Investigate

Judge

Justify

Launch

Lead

Lecture

License

Listen

Locate

Maintain

Manage

Manipulate

Manufacture

Map

Market

Mastermind

Measure

Mediate

Mentor

Model

Modify

Monitor

Motivate

Navigate

Negotiate

Nominate

Normalize

Observe

Obtain

Officiate

Operate

Orchestrate

Organize

Orient

Originate

Outsource

Overcome

Oversee

Participate

Perceive

Perfect

Perform

Persuade

Pilot

Pinpoint

Pioneer

Plan

Position

Predict

Prepare

Prescribe

Present

Preside

Process

Procure

Program

Progress

Project

Project manage

Promote

Propose

Prospect

Provide

Publicize

Purchase

Qualify

Question

Rate

Realign

Rebuild

Recapture

Receive

Recognize

Recommend

Reconcile

Record

Recruit

Redesign

Reduce

Reengineer

Regain

Regulate

Rehabilitate

Reinforce

Rejuvenate

Render

Renegotiate

Reorganize

Report

Reposition

Represent

Research

Resolve

Respond

Restore

Restructure

Retrieve

Review

Revise

Revitalize

Satisfy

Schedule

Secure

Select

Separate

Serve

Simplify

Sold

Solidify

Solve

Specify

Speak

Standardize

Stimulate

Streamline

Structure

Succeed	Transcribe
Suggest	Transfer
Summarize	Transform
Supervise	Transition
Supply	Translate
Support	Troubleshoot
Surpass	Unify
Synthesize	Unite
Systematize	Update
Tabulate	Upgrade
Target	Use
Teach	Utilize
Terminate	Verbalize
Test	Verify
Thwart	Win
Train	Write

HIGH-IMPACT PHRASES

Use these High-Impact Descriptive & Performance KeyWords to describe yourself, your personality, your leadership style, and your ability to impact organizational change and improvement.

Accelerated Career Track

Accelerating Revenue Growth

Aggressive Turnaround Leadership

Benchmarking

Best In Class

Business Process Redesign

Business Process Reengineering

Capturing Cost Reductions

Catalyst for Change

Change Agent

Change Management

Competitive Market Positioning

Competitive Wins

Competitively Positioning Products & Technologies

Contemporary Management Style

Core Competencies

Creative Business Leader

Creative Problem-Solver

Cross-Culturally Sensitive

Cross-Functional Expertise

Cross-Functional Team Leadership

Decisive Management Style

Delivering Strong and Sustainable Gains

Direct & Decisive Organizational Leadership

Distinguished Performance

Driving Customer Loyalty Initiatives

Driving Innovation

Driving Performance Improvement

Driving Productivity Gains

Emerging Business Ventures

Emerging International Markets

Entrepreneurial Drive

Entrepreneurial Leadership

Entrepreneurial Vision

Executive Leadership

Executive Liaison

Fast-Track Promotion

Global Market Dominance

High-Caliber

High-Growth

High-Impact

High-Performance

High-Quality

Matrix Management

Multi-Discipline Industry Expertise

Organizational Driver

Organizational Leader

Outperforming Global Competition

Outperforming Market Competition

PC Proficient

Peak Performer

Performance Improvement

Performance Management

Performance Reengineering

Pioneering Technologies

Proactive Business Leader

Proactive Manager

Process Redesign

Process Reengineering

Productivity Improvement

Self-Starter

Start-Up, Turnaround & High-Growth Organizations

Strategic & Tactical Operations

Strong & Sustainable Financial Gains

Strong & Sustainable Performance Gains

Strong & Sustainable Productivity Gains

Strong & Sustainable Profit Gains

Strong & Sustainable Quality Gains

Strong & Sustainable Technology Gains

Team Building

Team Leadership

Technologically Advanced Organization

Technologically Sophisticated Operations

Top Flight Leadership Competencies

Top Tier Executive

Visionary Leadership

World Class Leadership

World Class Operations

World Class Organization

PERSONALITY DESCRIPTORS

Use these Personality Descriptors to highlight your specific personal and professional attributes.

Abstract	Bilingual
Accurate	Bold
Action-Driven	Brave
Adaptable	Communicative
Adventures	Competent
Aggressive	Competitive
Amenable	Conceptual
Analytical	Confident
Artful	Conscientious
Assertive	Conservative
Believable	Cooperative

Courageous
Creative
Credible
Cross-Cultural
Culturally-Sensitive
Customer-Driven
Dauntless
Decisive
Dedicated
Dependable
Determined
Devoted
Diligent
Diplomatic
Direct
Dramatic
Driven
Dynamic
Eager
Earnest
Effective
Efficient
Eloquent
Employee-Driven
Empowered
Encouraging
Energetic
Energized
Enterprising
Enthusiastic

Entrepreneurial
Ethical
Experienced
Expert
Expressive
Forward-Thinking
Global
Hardworking
Healthy
Helpful
Heroic
High-Impact
High-Potential
Honest
Honorable
Humanistic
Humanitarian
Humorous
Immediate
Impactful
Important
Impressive
Incomparable
Individualistic
Industrious
Independent
Ingenious
Innovative
Insightful
Intelligent

Intense

Intuitive

Judicious

Keen

Leader

Loyal

Managerial

Market-Driven

Masterful

Mature

Mechanical

Methodical

Modern

Moral

Motivated

Motivational

Multilingual

Notable

Noteworthy

Objective

Observant

Opportunistic

Oratorical

Orderly

Organized

Outstanding

Participative

Participatory

Peerless

Perfectionist

Performance-Driven

Perservering

Persistent

Personable

Persuasive

Philosophical

Photogenic

Pioneering

Poised

Polished

Popular

Positive

Practical

Pragmatic

Precise

Preeminent

Prepared

Proactive

Problem-Solver

Productive

Professional

Proficient

Progressive

Prominent

Prudent

Punctual

Quality-Driven

Reactive

Reliable

Reputable

Resilient

Resourceful

Results-Driven

Results-Oriented

Savvy

Sensitive

Sharp

Skilled

Skillful

Sophisticated

Spirited

Strategic

Strong

Subjective

Successful

Tactful

Talented

Teacher

Team Builder

Team Leader

Team Player

Technical

Tenacious

Thorough

Tolerant

Top-Performer

Top-Producer

Traditional

Trainer

Trilingual

Trouble Shooter

Trustworthy

Truthful

Unrelenting

Understanding

Upbeat

Valiant

Valuable

Venturesome

Veracious

Verbal

Victorious

Vigorous

Virtuous

Visionary

Vital

Vivacious

Well-Balanced

Well-Versed

Winning

Wise

Wordly

Youthful

Zealous

Zestful

RESUME & JOB SEARCH RESOURCES

THE ADVANTAGE INC.

Executive Resume & Career Management Center

The Advantage, Inc., one of the nation's foremost resume and job search centers, was founded by Wendy S. Enelow in August 1986. The firm specializes in resume development, job search and career coaching for professional, management, senior management and executive job search candidates. To date, The Advantage has worked with more than 5000 professionals worldwide to plan and manage their successful job search campaigns!

Professional writers and coaches work one-on-one with you to explore your professional goals, develop career strategies, create winning resumes and implement action plans that competitively position you to:

> ## Win in Today's Competitive Job Search Market!

Executive Resume Development | Targeted Direct Mail
Cover Letter Writing Services | Internet Online Services
Executive Career Planning & Coaching | Interview Counseling
Executive Job Lead Publications | KeyWord Presentations

Consultations with Wendy Enelow are by scheduled appointment. If you are interested in executive resume, career coaching or job search management services, fax the form below with your resume to (804) 384-4700 or phone (804) 384-4600.

- -

❑   **YES!**   Please contact me regarding your services and pricing. My resume is attached.

NAME: _____

ADDRESS: _____

PHONE: _____

FAX: _____

CAREER RESOURCES

Contact Impact Publications for a free annotated listing of career resources or visit their World Wide Web site for a complete listing of career resources: ***http://www.impactpublications.com***
   The following career resources are available directly from Impact Publications. Complete this form or list the titles, include postage (see formula at the end), enclose payment, and send your order to:

IMPACT PUBLICATIONS
9104-N Manassas Drive
Manassas Park, VA 20111-5211
Tel. 703/361-7300 or Fax 703/335-9486
E-mail: impactp@impactpublications.com

Orders from individuals must be prepaid by check, moneyorder, Visa, MasterCard, or American Express. We accept telephone and fax orders.

Qty.	TITLES	Price	TOTAL
Resume Books			
____	100 Winning Resumes For $100,000+ Jobs	$24.95	_____
____	101 Best Resumes	$10.95	_____
____	101 Great Resumes	$9.99	_____
____	175 High-Impact Resumes	$10.95	_____
____	1500+ KeyWords for $100,000+ Jobs	$14.95	_____
____	Adams Resume Almanac	$10.95	_____
____	America's Top Resumes For America's Top Jobs	$19.95	_____
____	Asher's Bible of Executive Resumes	$29.95	_____
____	Best Resumes For $75,000+ Executive Jobs	$19.95	_____
____	Building a Great Resume	$15.00	_____
____	Complete Idiot's Guide to Crafting the Perfect Resume	$16.95	_____
____	Designing the Perfect Resume	$12.95	_____
____	Dynamite Resumes	$14.95	_____
____	Electronic Resumes: Putting Your Resume On-Line	$19.95	_____
____	Electronic Resumes For the New Job Market	$11.95	_____
____	Encyclopedia of Job-Winning Resumes	$16.95	_____
____	Gallery of Best Resumes	$16.95	_____
____	Gallery of Best Resumes For Two-Year Degree Graduates	$14.95	_____

___	High Impact Resumes and Letters	$19.95 ___
___	How to Prepare Your Curriculum Vitae	$14.95 ___
___	Internet Resumes	$14.95 ___
___	Just Resumes	$11.95 ___
___	NBEW's Resumes	$11.95 ___
___	New Perfect Resume	$10.95 ___
___	Portfolio Power	$14.95 ___
___	Power Resumes	$12.95 ___
___	Quick Resume and Cover Letter Book	$12.95 ___
___	Real-Life Resumes That Work!	$12.95 ___
___	Resume Catalog	$15.95 ___
___	Resume Pro	$24.95 ___
___	Resume Shortcuts	$14.95 ___
___	Resume Solution	$12.95 ___
___	Resume Winners From the Pros	$17.95 ___
___	Resume Writing Made Easy	$10.95 ___
___	Resumes & Job Search Letters For Transitioning Military Personnel	$17.95 ___
___	Resumes For Advertising Careers	$9.95 ___
___	Resumes For Architecture and Related Careers	$9.95 ___
___	Resumes For Banking and Financial Careers	$9.95 ___
___	Resumes For Business Management Careers	$9.95 ___
___	Resumes For Communications Careers	$9.95 ___
___	Resumes For Dummies	$12.99 ___
___	Resumes For Education Careers	$9.95 ___
___	Resumes For Engineering Careers	$9.95 ___
___	Resumes For Environmental Careers	$9.95 ___
___	Resumes For Ex-Military Personnel	$9.95 ___
___	Resumes For 50+ Job Hunters	$9.95 ___
___	Resumes For the Healthcare Professional	$12.95 ___
___	Resumes For High Tech Careers	$9.95 ___
___	Resumes For Midcareer Job Changers	$9.95 ___
___	Resumes For the Over 50 Job Hunter	$14.95 ___
___	Resumes For People Who Hate to Write Resumes	$12.95 ___
___	Resumes For Re-Entry: A Woman's Handbook	$10.95 ___
___	Resumes For Sales and Marketing Careers	$9.95 ___
___	Resumes For Scientific and Technical Careers	$9.95 ___
___	Resumes in Cyberspace	$14.95 ___
___	Resumes That Knock 'Em Dead	$10.95 ___
___	Resumes, Resumes, Resumes	$9.99 ___
___	Sure-Hire Resumes	$14.95 ___

Resume Books With Computer Disk

___	Adams Resume Almanac With Disk	$19.95 ___
___	New 90-Minute Resume	$15.95 ___
___	Ready-to-Go Resumes	$16.95 ___

Resume CD-ROMs

___	Adams JobBank Fast Resume Suite	$49.95 ___
___	ResumeMaker	$49.95 ___
___	Win-Way Resume 4.0	$69.95 ___

Resume Software (specify disk size and system)

___	Perfect Resume Kit (Individual Version)	$49.95 ___
___	Perfect Resume Kit (Counselor Version)	$259.95 ___
___	Perfect Resume Kit (Lab Pack Version)	$639.95 ___
___	Perfect Resume Kit (Network Version)	$999.95 ___

Cover Letters

___	175 High-Impact Cover Letters	$10.95 ___
___	200 Letters For Job Hunters	$19.95 ___
___	201 Dynamite Job Search Letters	$19.95 ___
___	201 Killer Cover Letters	$16.95 ___
___	201 Winning Cover Letters For $100,000+ Jobs	$24.95 ___
___	Adams Cover Letter Almanac and Disk	$19.95 ___
___	Cover Letters For Dummies	$12.99 ___
___	Cover Letters That Knock 'Em Dead	$10.95 ___
___	Cover Letters, Cover Letters, Cover Letters	$9.95 ___
___	Dynamite Cover Letters	$14.95 ___
___	NBEW's Cover Letters	$11.95 ___
___	Perfect Cover Letter	$10.95 ___
___	Sure-Hire Cover Letters	$10.95 ___

Interviews, Networking, and Salary Negotiations

___	101 Dynamite Answers to Interview Questions	$12.95 ___
___	101 Dynamite Questions to Ask At Your Job Interview	$14.95 ___
___	101 Dynamite Ways to Ace Your Job Interview	$13.95 ___
___	201 Answers to the Toughest Job Interview Questions	$10.95 ___
___	Adams Job Interview Almanacs	$10.95 ___
___	Ask the Headhunter	$14.95 ___
___	Dynamite Networking For Dynamite Jobs	$15.95 ___
___	Dynamite Salary Negotiation	$15.95 ___
___	Great Connections	$19.95 ___
___	How to Work a Room	$9.95 ___
___	Interview For Success	$15.95 ___
___	Interview Kit	$10.95 ___
___	Interview Power	$12.95 ___
___	Job Interviews For Dummies	$12.99 ___
___	NBEW's Interviewing	$11.95 ___
___	Power Schmoozing	$12.95 ___
___	Quick Interview and Salary Negotiation Book	$12.95 ___
___	The Secrets of Savvy Networking	$11.99 ___
___	What Do I Say Next?	$20.00 ___

Skills, Testing, Self-Assessment, Empowerment

___	7 Habits of Highly Effective People	$14.00 ___
___	Career Satisfaction and Success	$9.95 ___
___	Chicken Soup For the Soul	$12.95 ___
___	Discover the Best Jobs For You	$15.95 ___
___	Do What You Are	$16.95 ___
___	Do What You Love, the Money Will Follow	$10.95 ___

___ Get a Job You Love!	$19.95	___
___ Gifts Differing	$14.95	___
___ Love Your Work and Success Will Follow	$12.95	___
___ P.I.E. Method For Career Success	$14.95	___
___ Real People, Real Jobs	$15.95	___
___ A Second Helping of Chicken Soup For the Soul	$12.95	___
___ Starting Out, Starting Over	$14.95	___
___ A Third Helping of Chicken Soup For the Soul	$12.95	___

Dress, Appearing, Image

___ 110 Mistakes Working Women Make and How to Avoid Them: Dressing Smart in the 90's	$9.95	___
___ John Molloy's New Dress For Success (men)	$12.99	___
___ The New Women's Dress For Success	$12.99	___
___ Red Socks Don't Work! (men)	$14.95	___
___ The Winning Image	$17.95	___

Job Search Strategies and Tactics

___ 101 Great Answers to the Toughest Job Search Problems	$11.99	___
___ 110 Biggest Mistakes Job Hunters Make	$19.95	___
___ 303 Off the Wall Ways to Get a Job	$12.99	___
___ Change Your Job, Change Your Life	$17.95	___
___ Complete Job Finder's Guide to the 90s	$13.95	___
___ Dynamite Tele-Search	$12.95	___
___ Five Secrets to Finding a Job	$12.95	___
___ How to Get Interviews From Classified Job Ads	$14.95	___
___ Job Hunter's Catalog	$10.95	___
___ Job Hunting For Dummies	$16.99	___
___ Joyce Lain Kennedy's Career Book	$29.95	___
___ Knock 'Em Dead	$12.95	___
___ New Rites of Passage At $100,000+	$29.95	___
___ Professional's Job Finder	$18.95	___
___ Strategic Job Jumping	$13.00	___
___ What Color Is Your Parachute?	$16.95	___

Electronic Job Search and the Internet

___ Adams Electronic Job Search Almanac 1998	$9.95	___
___ Be Your Own Headhunter	$16.00	___
___ CareerXroads: 500 Best Sites on WWW	$22.95	___
___ Electronic Job Search Revolution	$12.95	___
___ Employer's Guide to Recruiting on the Internet	$24.95	___
___ Finding a Job on the Internet	$16.95	___
___ Getting on the Information Superhighway	$11.95	___
___ Guide to Internet Job Searching	$14.95	___
___ Hook Up, Get Hired	$12.95	___
___ How to Get Your Dream Job Using the Web	$29.99	___
___ Point and Click Jobfinder	$14.95	___
___ The Three R's of E-Mail	$12.95	___
___ Using the Internet & the World Wide Web in Your Job Search	$16.95	___

Best Jobs and Employers

___	100 Best Careers For the 21st Century	$15.95 ___
___	American Almanac of Jobs and Salaries	$17.00 ___
___	Best Jobs For the 21st Century	$19.95 ___
___	Hidden Job Market 1998	$18.95 ___
___	Jobs 1998	$15.00 ___

Key Directories

___	American Salaries and Wages Survey	$105.00 ___
___	The Big Book of Minority Opportunities	$39.95 ___
___	Business Phone Book USA	$135.00 ___
___	Complete Guide For Occupational Exploration	$39.95 ___
___	Dictionary of Occupational Titles	$39.95 ___
___	Directory of Executive Recruiters (annual)	$44.95 ___
___	Encyclopedia of Careers and Vocational Guidance	$149.95 ___
___	Enhanced Guide For Occupational Exploration	$34.95 ___
___	Free and Inexpensive Career Materials	$19.95 ___
___	Internships (annual)	$24.95 ___
___	Job Hunter's Sourcebook	$70.00 ___
___	National Trade and Professional Associations	$85.00 ___
___	Minority Organizations	$49.95 ___
___	Occupational Outlook Handbook	$21.95 ___
___	Professional Careers Sourcebook	$99.95 ___

International, Overseas, and Travel Jobs

___	Careers in International Affairs	$17.95 ___
___	Complete Guide to International Jobs & Careers	$13.95 ___
___	International Jobs Directory	$19.95 ___
___	Jobs For People Who Love Travel	$15.95 ___
___	Jobs in Russia and the Newly Independent States	$15.95 ___
___	Jobs Worldwide	$17.95 ___
___	Teaching English Abroad	$15.95 ___

Public-Oriented Careers

___	Complete Guide to Public Employment	$19.95 ___
___	Directory of Federal Jobs and Employers	$21.95 ___
___	Federal Applications That Get Results	$23.95 ___
___	Federal Jobs in Law Enforcement	$14.95 ___
___	Find a Federal Job Fast!	$15.95 ___
___	Government Job Finder	$16.95 ___
___	Jobs and Careers With Nonprofit Organizations	$15.95 ___
___	Jobs For Lawyers	$14.95 ___
___	Non-Profit's Job Finder	$16.95 ___

Videos

___	Attitude!	$149.00 ___
___	Chicken Soup For the Soul Video Series	$59.95 ___
___	Dialing For Jobs	$139.00 ___

___	Dynamite Interview Questions and Techniques	$149.95	_____
___	How to Present a Professional Image (2 videos)	$149.95	_____
___	The Miracle Résumé	$99.00	_____
___	The Video Résumé Writer	$102.95	_____

Military

___	From Air Force Blue to Corporate Gray	$17.95	_____
___	From Army Green to Corporate Gray	$17.95	_____
___	From Navy Blue to Corporate Gray	$17.95	_____
___	Jobs and the Military Spouse	$14.95	_____
___	Résumés & Job Search Letters For Transitioning Military Personnel	$17.95	_____

CD-ROMs

___	America's Top Jobs	$295.00	_____
___	Encyclopedia of Associations	$595.00	_____
___	Encyclopedia of Careers and Vocational Guidance	$199.95	_____
___	Ultimate Job Source	$199.95	_____

SUBTOTAL --- _____

Virginia residents add 4½% sales tax   _____

POSTAGE/HANDLING ($5.00 for first
title plus 8% of SUBTOTAL over $30) $5.00

8% of SUBTOTAL over $30--- _____

TOTAL ENCLOSED ------------------------------------- _____

NAME _____

ADDRESS _____

_____

_____

❑ I enclose check/moneyorder for $ _____ made payable to
IMPACT PUBLICATIONS.

❑ Please charge $ _____ to my credit card:

❑ Visa   ❑ MasterCard   ❑ American Express

Card # _____

Expiration date: _____/_____

Signature _____

The On-Line Superstore & Warehouse

Hundreds of Terrific Career Resources Conveniently Available On the World Wide Web 24-Hours a Day, 365 Days a Year!

Ever wanted to know what are the newest and best books, directories, newsletters, wall charts, training programs, videos, CD-ROMs, computer software, and kits available to help you land a job, negotiate a higher salary, or start your own business? What about finding a job in Asia or relocating to San Francisco? Are you curious about how to find a job 24-hours a day by using the Internet or what you'll be doing five years from now? Trying to keep up-to-date on the latest career resources but not able to find the latest catalogs, brochures, or newsletters on today's "best of the best" resources?

Welcome to the first virtual career bookstore on the Internet. Now you're only a "click" away with Impact Publication's electronic solution to the resource challenge. Impact Publications, one of the nation's leading publishers and distributors of career resources, has launched its comprehensive "Career Superstore and Warehouse" on the Internet. The bookstore is jam-packed with the latest job and career resources on:

- Alternative jobs and careers
- Self-assessment
- Career planning and job search
- Employers
- Relocation and cities
- Resumes
- Cover Letters
- Dress, image, and etiquette
- Education
- Telephone
- Military
- Salaries
- Interviewing
- Nonprofits
- Empowerment
- Self-esteem
- Goal setting
- Executive recruiters
- Entrepreneurship
- Government
- Networking
- Electronic job search
- International jobs
- Travel
- Law
- Training and presentations
- Minorities
- Physically challenged

The bookstore also includes a new "Military Career Transition Center" and "School-to-Work Center."

"This is more than just a bookstore offering lots of product," say Drs. Ron and Caryl Krannich, two of the nation's leading career experts and authors and developers of this on-line bookstore. *"We're an important resource center for libraries, corporations, government, educators, trainers, and career counselors who are constantly defining and redefining this dynamic field. Of the thousands of career resources we review each year, we only select the 'best of the best.'"*

Visit this rich site and you'll quickly discover just about everything you ever wanted to know about finding jobs, changing careers, and starting your own business—including many useful resources that are difficult to find in local bookstores and libraries. The site also includes what's new and hot, tips for job search success, and monthly specials. Impact's Web address is:

http://www.impactpublications.com